I Met Jesus

for a

Miller Lite

Danny Bader

Foreword by Father Michael Connolly, O.S.F.S

http://www.dannybader.com

ISBN-13: 978-0-692-09317-7

Dedication

*To Mom, Dad, Trish, Paul, Eddie, Mick, Matt,
Tim & Kevin ... luv ya!*

*And to all of us on this spiritual journey
called Life; may we always come back to the
message. . .*

Foreword

I first met Danny Bader—*not* for a Miller Lite!—35 years ago when he was a student at the university where I was teaching. We have kept in contact for all these years since then.

Danny's first book, *Back from Heaven's Front Porch*, was clearly autobiographical. Danny's newest book *I Met Jesus for a Miller Lite* is somewhat autobiographical but still fiction. It is a fanciful tale—not theology—but with profound underlying spiritual truths often manifested in the ordinary events of any life.

Danny's principal characters reveal great sensitivity to a human's inherent access to God—here specifically in the person of Jesus Christ. Discipleship and intimate friendship with Jesus are two sides of the same reality.

For all of us on the spiritual journey called life, this book—peppered with humor, empathy, tears and laughter: the full gamut of human emotions—is an invitation to explore our spiritual friendship with Jesus and the implications of that discipleship for our values and behaviors.

The story's ending comes as a startling surprise—but, in retrospect, not entirely! This book leaves the reader with a softened heart and hopefully with a more determined will to look for Jesus in unlikely places and among unlikely fellow sojourners, perhaps even in your own favorite "watering hole." Cheers!

Father Michael C. Connolly, O.S.F.S.

Contents

Chapter 1: The Hit 1

Chapter 2: The Void 7

Chapter 3: The Call 17

Chapter 4: The Problem 27

Chapter 5: The Thoughts 39

Chapter 6: The Stranger 49

Chapter 7: The Turndown 61

Chapter 8: The Past 75

Chapter 9: The Serendipity 85

Chapter 10: The Second Chance 93

Chapter 11: The Return 101

Chapter 12: The Questions 107

Chapter 13: The Realization 113

Chapter 14: The Choice 121

Chapter 15: The Fear 143

Chapter 16: The Riddle 159

Chapter 17: The Healing 165

Chapter 18: The Trust 175

Epilogue: A Mere Breath 191

CHAPTER 1

The Hit

Growth lies not at the top of the climb;
it's gathered on the way up.

The last NFL preseason game was over. I was alone in the locker room, seated in front of the locker that had a black plate screwed to the top with white numbers and letters: 33 TRUMBALL 33.

The uniforms had been taken away to be washed. The smell of defeat lingered in the air mixed with cologne. My head felt like it was filled with cement. I took a deep breath and stood, the damp towel wrapped around my waist, drops of water still falling from my hair. The equipment manager stopped on his way out, his smile revealing bright teeth against dark skin. "Don't beat yourself up, Michael. It's all gonna be OK." I wasn't sure about that.

I looked at myself in the mirror, noticing the black under my eye and the muscular 6-foot, 210-pound man staring back. My head started to swim and I sat back down, scanning through my clouded thoughts for the memory. It had been near the end of the third quarter and our quarterback called the play in the huddle—a screen pass to me. The ball was snapped and I moved to my right, blocking the oncoming rusher just enough to slow him down. Then I moved toward the right sideline, turning back to see the quarterback sidestep the player I'd just blocked and float the ball my way. The ball landed gently in my grasp as I turned to head down the field. I think I only took one step before I was hit from the left side. It felt like a bus had run a stop sign, but I held onto that ball like my life depended on it. My helmet went flying toward the players on the sideline.

I had a brief thought, *This is it.* As I slipped into blackness, I could swear I heard a voice saying, "Not yet."

The next thing I knew, I was in the blue tent on the sideline with our team doctor shining a light in my eye and holding up his finger, moving it from side to side. "We were really worried about you there for a minute, Michael," the doc said. "You were so still. . . ." He stopped speaking and swallowed. His next words were spoken with a much lighter tone. "I think they had to wrestle the ball from your grip even though you were unconscious."

I was cleared from a concussion, thankfully avoiding what would have been my third one; the doctor said it's extremely rare to be knocked out and not suffer a concussion. But I sat on the sidelines the rest of the game, watching all the other guys competing for a spot on the team play their guts out.

After the game, I lingered while the rest of the team hit the showers. All of them were gone now. I just kept sitting there. The irony of escaping a third concussion hit me. Here I was trying out for what would become my third team in five years with the NFL. I'd started a few games for the first team, but played mostly on the special teams and as a backup.

Probably won't be starting any games here now, I thought as I finished dressing and tucked my necktie in the leather bag, not having the energy to put it on.

The running backs coach stopped by. He was a young guy, about the same size as me, and we got along OK. Like me, he'd been in the league five years. In a soft voice, his eyes avoiding mine, he said, "Hey, Michael, come in tomorrow morning before practice. The coach wants to see you."

I nodded, then headed for the parking lot. "Goodnight, Michael," the security guard said from his desk by the exit door. I smiled slightly and exited, welcoming the cool air on my face as I battled what felt like a brutal hangover. My black Jeep sat alone toward the rear. Its lights flashed as I pressed the remote and then slid behind the wheel.

Several teammates had invited me over to a steakhouse in The Gulch section of Nashville, but I wasn't up for that. All I could think about was the disaster that had happened the last time I'd gone there.

We'd finished training camp and begun the preseason when Jackie, my girlfriend through high school and college, called and said she and her friend Susan were coming to Nashville for a long weekend and wanted to get together. I was looking forward to seeing Jackie, who was perhaps more friend than girlfriend. She was living back in our hometown and had made it clear that with me moving around following my dream, we seemed to be "going nowhere" in our relationship. I remember how beautiful she'd looked that night, the open windows behind the back bar raised and allowing the cool August air to blow softly as the city skyline glowed a few miles away. Her tight jeans hugged slender legs, tucked into worn black cowboy boots, and the blond-streaked hair that I'd loved from the first day I saw her hung in a simple pony tail down the back of her white silk blouse.

Susan, her friend, was a few barstools down, smiling coyly at Tom, one of my teammates. The thing with Susan was that her smile was more the product of the martini in front of her—or the one or two she already had—than it was the result of her present state in life.

Jackie and I were discussing my chances of making the Nashville team this year.

"The guy in front of me has played really well and I know our coach likes him because they drafted him. Plus, the starter should be back from a sprained knee in a few weeks for the season opener." I fiddled with my glass. "But I've never shied away from hard work and

I'll play as hard as I can to show them I can do the job. I'm confident everything will work out."

Jackie smiled. "That's one of the things I've always envied about you, Michael. Your devotion to football and commitment to doing whatever it takes to succeed is really admirable."

I was going to reply when we heard Susan laughing and turned to see her talking with a woman I recognized as Tom's wife. She turned her back on Susan, said a few harsh words to her husband, and walked out. Tom, a full head taller than Susan, leaned down and whispered something to her before making his way through the crowd after his wife. I shook my head. "Jack, she's a mess. She looks like she's been partying for a month. Why'd you have to bring her?"

"Michael, trust me, you'd do the same for one of your friends if they were hurting like Susan. I know she's got some problems now." She looked to Susan, now smiling and talking to the couple next to her. "But she's working on it and I have to support her as best I can."

"Well, she ought to just begin by stopping drinking. How's that for a start?" I said sarcastically.

We grabbed Susan and went into the dining room. She flirted with the waiter—and kept ordering martinis—throughout the meal. After I paid the check, we walked to the front door. Susan stopped and surprised the waiter with a kiss on the cheek as he stood in front of a glowing computer screen. She began to whisper in his ear until Jackie gently pulled her away. I offered to give them a ride back to their hotel, but Susan insisted on heading out to hear some music. Jackie gave me a kiss on the cheek as Susan sat on the front steps fiddling with her phone. "Good luck," I said, rolling my eyes. "Maybe see you tomorrow?"

She smiled sadly and looked toward Susan. "Thanks. I need to get her home soon."

About four hours later my phone buzzed, waking me from a deep sleep. I didn't recognize the number, but it was local so I thought I'd answer. "Hello."

The voice was filled with anger and talking fast. "Michael. This is Jennifer, and I'm sorry to wake you, I got your number from one of the other guys." It was Tom's wife, whom I'd seen at the steakhouse. My mind raced, wondering why she was calling so late. "Tom's not home yet and I'm wondering if you've seen him. I'm not getting anything back when I call and text him."

I stumbled through a sentence as I shook my head to become more conscious. "No, Jennifer, no, I've, uhh, I've not seen him since dinner."

"Shit, I was hoping maybe he was with you." She paused, then continued in an accusatory tone. "You're not with your friends from the restaurant, are you?"

"No, I'm at home. I—" I stopped talking when I heard a noise in the background through the phone.

Jennifer spoke, but not to me. "You son of a . . ." was the last thing I heard as the call was dropped.

I was going to text Jackie right then but decided to go back to sleep. After several restless hours I sat up in bed, reached for my phone, and sent a text to Jackie to see if she wanted to grab coffee before I went to practice. We met for about 45 minutes and I got the whole story. Apparently, Susan had given Tom her number and, unbeknownst to Jackie, had arranged to meet him at a well-known nightclub. She and Tom had danced and drank . . . and kept drinking. They left together, followed by a private investigator with a camera. The shit storm that followed was the last thing I needed. Jackie and Susan left town the next day, and I settled into the final weeks of preseason.

So, no, I didn't want to meet the team at that same steakhouse. Instead, I sat in my car in the stadium parking lot, telling myself that I'd played well enough in the other preseason games to make the team.

For the first time in my life, I wasn't sure I believed it.

CHAPTER 2

The Void

We must sail sometimes with the wind and sometimes against it—but we must sail, and not drift, nor lie at anchor.
- Oliver Wendell Holmes

The next morning, I dressed in my team sweatpants and hoodie and made the drive to the practice complex. A text from my mom came in, saying she wanted to talk later to hear what was happening now that the preseason was over. She reminded me that the ladies at church were all praying for me; and as always she ended her text with "so proud of you, luv ya."

I pulled into the parking lot an hour before practice, making sure I was there for the meeting that the head coach had requested. Our equipment manager was sipping a cup of coffee as I walked through the doors and turned left, away from the locker room and toward the coach's office. He smiled slightly and nodded. "Morning, Michael."

The coach's door was closed. His assistant, a stocky woman typing away on her laptop, looked up and greeted me. "Hi, Michael. Coach will be with you in a few minutes. You can just have a seat."

"Thanks." I took a seat, my mouth dry and stomach tight. I thought about texting my mom or my best friend, Nick, but before I could make that decision, the door opened and out walked a veteran linebacker who'd played with Tennessee the past eight seasons.

He walked by me, patting my shoulder, "Good luck, brother." I stood, nodding quickly. "Thanks. You too." He stopped to give the lady at the desk a hug, as she motioned with her head for me to enter the coach's office.

It was a short meeting; I knew from experience they usually were. The coach first asked me how I felt. "That was a nasty hit you took last night. Not sure anyone else could've held onto the ball on that one." I began to reply, but he interrupted, thanking me for my commitment during camp and preseason, then saying he'd decided to let me go from the team and that he wished me all the best in life.

When I asked about staying around to be on the practice squad, he just shook his head. "You may want to have your agent check in with Cleveland and the Jets. I know they've been looking around for some backs." I shook his hand. We exchanged pleasantries, and for the third time in my short NFL career I walked out of a head coach's office to go clean out my locker.

I made sure to keep my usual look of confidence plastered on my face as I entered the locker room. It was clear all the guys knew, and I received handshakes and words of encouragement from most. I opened my locker and saw that the team playbook and all of my equipment was gone. No more "33 Trumball" on anything. I tossed my few personal items into my backpack, threw it over my shoulder and stood for a moment, staring at the blank space where only yesterday a plate had hung with my name and number on it. *I wonder whose name will go up there next.*

One of the rookies, who obviously had made the cut, stopped by in his workout gear. "Hey, man, sorry about you getting cut. I wanted to thank you for being such a great mentor to me these past two months." He held out his hand, and we shook. "I like all the guys on the team, but you're the one who really took time out to help me adjust to being here and play to my best ability."

"No sweat, Ron. And just remember to play the game the way that feels right to you. Don't let anyone force you to try to be someone else. You've got the goods as long as you focus on playing to your strengths."

"Appreciate the comment, man. And if there's ever anything I can do, just ask. I'm not sure I'd be sticking around if it weren't for you."

As I drove toward my apartment, the empty feeling inside was eased some by Ron's words. I'd really enjoyed working with him. I decided not to get off at my usual exit, succumbing to some invisible force that led me out to winding backcountry roads. A mantra played over and over in my mind. *No more pro football. No more pro football.*

I stopped for gas at a convenience store, grabbed a Gatorade, and sat on a bench in a small picnic area next to the parking lot. My thoughts whirled. *What am I gonna do now? I guess my career—if I can call it that—is over. Or maybe I could get some private coaching, work harder on my drills, and try out for another team. Should I go to Canada? I'm pretty sure I'd get more playing time up there.*

I called my agent, but he didn't answer so I left a voicemail asking him to call me back. I did not tell him I'd been cut, as he'd known about both other times before me. I guessed he had his sources on the inside. My phone buzzed and I saw a text from my mom.

> Hi honey, just thinking of you and looking forward
> to talking later today. I know you're probably busy at
> practice so no need to text me back. Luv ya.

My mom was on my mind, and I was not looking forward to telling her, although she'd likely be relieved; she'd commented after my second concussion that I should stop playing and come home. "Your health is the most important thing to me," she always said.

Everybody knows about the dangers of concussions these days. But ever since I was 8 years old, I just knew I was going to play in the

NFL for 10 years. My mind couldn't seem to grasp that I was going to come up six years short.

I was going to text my mom back out of habit, but then realized she'd wonder—or she'd probably know—why I wasn't at practice. My phone buzzed again.

> Hey man. I heard about this morning. Let's stay positive.
> I talked with the player personnel guy and he told me
> about Cleveland. I've got a call in to them. Got a crazy
> busy day here. I'll be in touch.

I shook my head at the text from my agent. *I'm sure he's crazy busy with clients that don't get cut. He's got to make a living too.* But at the same time, I knew we'd have to act quickly if I was to get a shot at making another team. I texted back:

> OK. Talk later.

My stomach growled. I drove home, parked the car, and walked a few blocks to a nearby sports bar to grab lunch and a few beers. As I walked through the front door, I could see the servers scuttling around in assorted NFL jerseys.

I took a seat at the bar and ordered a beer and hot pork sandwich. The lunch crowd was steady, mostly tourists in cowboy boots and hats. I had a brief exchange about Nashville's chances this year with a guy wearing jeans and a blazer. I was certain he had no idea who I was. *And why would he? A no-name preseason player who didn't make the cut.*

As I ate my barbecue-sauce-dripping pork sandwich, I was blessed with the gift of ESPN covering all the NFL cuts as the teams scrambled and strategized to get down to their 53-man roster. I saw my name come up and ordered another beer. And maybe another one after that. Somewhere in the middle of my self-indulgence, I talked with my agent, who was very upbeat about my prospects.

A few hours later I walked home and took a nap. I called my mom when I woke up. "Hey, mom."

"Oh, hi, honey. I've been so excited to talk with you. How are you?" I imagined her smile as she sat in her favorite blue chair in the sunroom at her house. The past two times I'd had this call with my mom I spent a few minutes in small talk with her, but this time was different.

I got up from the couch, holding the phone in one hand and running the other through my hair. "Mom, I got cut this morning." There was a pause, then some sniffles.

"Oh, Michael, I'm so sorry. But maybe this is a sign, you know. That hit you took yesterday was awful. Maybe it's time you started using that finance degree you got in college or those broadcasting skills you've been working on."

I interrupted her. "Mom, I know you're concerned. But I don't think I'm ready to give up yet. I talked with my agent and he thinks I can get a tryout with the Jets and maybe Cleveland. And I've made a lot of friends around the league. I'm going to make some calls and see if there are other opportunities out there in pro ball."

There was silence for a few seconds, then she spoke in a somber voice, "OK, honey. I understand. I'll support you in whatever you want to do next."

I began to talk, then stopped, suppressing my anger and frustration. She waited to see if I would fill in the silence. I didn't; she did. "Maybe you should come home for awhile. Let's talk later, OK? And know I love you."

After a deep breath, I responded. "Yep, sounds good. And I love you too, mom."

I didn't do much the rest of the afternoon. I tried calling Nick again, but got his voicemail. I didn't leave a message. I was trusting he'd see the missed call and call me back. Though come to think of it,

I'd tried calling him three times in the past week and hadn't gotten a response. Not even a text. When we'd last talked, I could sense he was distracted, asking the same question twice about the starting running back.

Nick and I had been friends for 20 years, ever since that first day we walked into Visitation grade school. I'll always remember that day, when so many kids were crying and upset, and Nick and I just drank chocolate milk and talked about playing dodge ball at recess. We finished our grade school years, then shared a quick four years in high school. He decided to go to school in the South and major in finance, while I remained close to home in the Northeast and I guess majored in football—at least I know I spent more time on that than on my studies. Now he was married to a wonderful woman named Anna, and I . . . well . . . let's just say I'm in transition with Jackie.

I didn't have much time to spend thinking about Nick, though. The next two weeks were a blur. I got a lot of calls from current and formers players I'd made friends with as I'd bounced around the league. We commiserated about how tough it was to stay at the top of the game. Some of them even gave me some leads on potential jobs. Most suggested I get out of football.

But one picked up on something my mom had said—that I should think about going into broadcasting. "You've got the looks, man," he said. "And you're smart and can talk intelligently about the game. Though that doesn't seem to be a requirement for most announcers!" We laughed as I agreed with him, intrigued by the possibility.

"You know, DaVon, I hadn't really considered that right now. But maybe you're right; I love to talk about the game. And being in broadcasting would keep me around the league—probably a lot longer than any playing career."

"That's right, kid. Plus I got three more words for you."

"Let me have it."

"Chicks dig it," said DaVon. "You're a handsome guy, and your face could be plastered over every TV in America, man. How else are you going to get a date?"

I was still laughing as we hung up.

I did manage to connect with Nick a few times, but he always seemed distracted. I didn't press it, figuring if he had something to tell me, he'd speak up when the time was right.

While this time should have felt like a new beginning, it felt like an old ending. I seemed to end up wandering around my apartment at all hours of the day and night. No more twice-daily workouts. No practice sessions. No locker rooms. No rigid attention to diet. None of the attention that pro players get. No more . . . me.

Fortunately for my self-esteem, I did get a workout with the Jets. But that's all I got, a workout. They thanked me for coming in and wished me well. No other teams contacted my agent, and I decided not to renew the next month on my apartment. I called around and nobody had any openings on practice squads. *Maybe I hear Canada calling*, I thought to myself.

Ironically, the next day a former teammate called to tell me about a team in Canada interested in talking with me. He said the general manager had graduated from State a few years before I played and had always kept an eye on my career. He didn't have an immediate opening, but he was worried about his team's current running back and wondered if I could go up for a tryout. I called the number my friend gave me and arranged a visit three days later. The people were great, I had a strong workout, and the money was good.

"Our roster's set for this year, but we are definitely interested in bringing on new talent," the GM told me. "How about this. You stay in shape over the winter and we'll consider having you join us at training camp next spring. No promises. It will all be up to you."

I'd been hoping for something more positive, but guessed I'd have to be patient. I plastered on a smile and shook the GM's hand, telling him I'd be ready come spring. *This is OK. I'll go home to Pennsylvania for a while, work hard over winter, and go to their camp next spring. Maybe play there for a year or two, and then get back to the NFL to finish my career. That will give me some time to start looking into this broadcasting thing, too.*

The line for international flights was long and moved slowly. The burly agent looked at me from head to toe when he saw I was a football player. He stamped my passport with a thud, handing it back to me with a solemn face. "No fumbles, eh?"

I took my passport. "Right."

I was feeling good as I settled into a chair by the gate, surrounded by women and men in business attire. I needed to call my mom, but instead decided to try Nick first. The phone rang several times, finally going to his voicemail. My stomach tightened and I pursed my lips as I listened to his familiar voicemail greeting. I left a message asking how he was and telling him to call me whenever he could. I stared at a sign written in both English and French, and realized I'd probably not be back to Canada any time soon.

When I landed in the States, I turned on my phone and saw I had a voicemail.

"Michael, it's Nick. Seems like we've been missing each other. I'm real busy with work and, um, some other stuff. Your mom said you might be coming back home. Give me a call if you do. Gotta go. Catch you later."

I tried calling Nick back, but again got no answer. So I sent him a short text.

Got your message. Hope all is well. Talk soon.

Deep down, I wondered what was going on with Nick. As far as I knew, his job and marriage were going great, but this was unlike him to be so hard to reach. Maybe the universe was sending me a message that I really did need to go home.

CHAPTER 3

The Call

*When the unpredictability of life shows up,
acceptance often precedes action.*

A week later, I was in my hometown in Pennsylvania, going with my mom and a real estate agent friend of hers to look at a house. I'd told Mom that I wasn't sure where I would land, but she was insistent about having me settle in Pennsylvania someday. "And besides, you're going to get tired of staying with me," she chided. "Wouldn't it be great to have a place of your own just a few miles from me? My friend Mary always tells me when there's a house on the market that she thinks you'd like!"

So I'd given in. And I must admit I liked the look of the four-bedroom stone-and-wood house. It was on a large corner lot in a nice neighborhood with tree-lined streets. It was older and needed some work, but it had a great stone patio in the backyard that had an outdoor fireplace and faced west toward the woods that defined the property line about 50 yards away.

I was tempted more than I thought I'd be, but visions of an NFL career still danced in my brain. So I had to tell my mom's friend the truth. "I really like the house, Mary, but I'm really not in a position to commit at the moment."

I dropped my mom off at her house then headed out. This was the first Friday since I'd moved back from Nashville. I'd finally talked to Nick, and we had plans to meet for dinner at one of our favorite places.

As I drove, I kept the windows rolled down, enjoying the cool night with its promise of the approaching winter. I was about 10 minutes from Harry's bar when my phone lit up, showing Nick's name. I was looking forward to seeing him because he'd been out of town on business when I arrived earlier that week. We'd talked a few times by phone and text, and he'd said he was very supportive of whatever choice I ended up making. I could tell something wasn't quite right with him, but didn't know what. Sometimes with your best friends, you just know.

"Hey, Nick! I'm just about there. Can't wait to see you and catch up!" I said, wondering if he was going to tell me he was running late.

"Hey, Michael." He paused. "I guess you're close to Harry's?" He had that odd sound in his voice again.

"Yep, a few minutes away. Everything OK?"

There was another pause, the kind that causes you to reach over and turn the radio down. Nick began to cry. "No, uhh, no, not good at all." He took a deep breath. "It's Anna. I've been meaning to tell you, but I just couldn't find the right time, and I wanted you to focus on the preseason."

I listened as he swallowed then spoke again in a strained voice. "She's had a lot of doctor appointments this past month, and we thought everything was OK, maybe just some minor woman stuff she had to get taken care of." Nick sighed. "Well, it's not. Michael, Anna has cancer."

I'm guessing you've had moments in life that you'll remember forever. I pulled my Jeep to the side of the road and parked. "What? Come on, man, this can't be. She looked phenomenal just before I left for camp. She was telling me how she was feeling so strong with her training for the Rocky Run in November."

Nick was silent, then took another deep breath. "I know. It's all real hard to believe. I mean here we just get married in the spring, get our house, and are ready to head off into our life together. . . ." His voice trailed off. I knew he was still there, and I stayed quiet, giving him some space.

He continued, "I was gonna tell you tonight in person. But we decided we really had to talk with our parents. They're on their way over now. So I can't meet you at Harry's."

"Yeah, uh, yeah, sure, buddy. Do your parents know?"

"Probably not her dad, but her mom knows something's up. She's been texting Anna a lot more than normal. I don't think my parents have a clue."

Now it was me who was taking a deep breath. "Well, what are the doctors saying? What kind is it? Does she need treatment now?" No sooner had I finished than I realized those were not the questions I should have been asking. Nick was silent, and I jumped in. "Shit, Nick, I'm sorry. I can only imagine what's going on for you in your head. What can I do? Should I come over?"

"No, it's OK, Michael. We're gonna keep this night for just our parents. We found out earlier this week, when Anna's doctor called a meeting. I jumped on the next flight home, and we've just been alone together for the past few days. We wanted to hold off telling family and friends until we knew more about what her treatment was going to look like, and we just kind of got our heads around all this. I'll let you know what happens tonight, and maybe we can get together tomorrow. Let's just see." He paused. "I know you'd like to come over, but. . . ."

I stopped him. "You've got much more important things to worry about, buddy. I'll be fine tonight. I won't tell anyone. Text me later if you can, just a quick one. And give Anna a hug from me, and tell her I'll be praying."

"Thanks, I'll give her a hug for sure. And it's OK to tell your mom and even Jackie if you talk with her. I'm sure word will spread fast, but we didn't want her parents to hear the gossip before we had a chance to talk to them."

"I understand. I'll see you or at least talk to you tomorrow then. Bye. Luv ya, Nick."

"Yep, love you too, Michael." He paused.

"Everything's going to be OK, Nick." I kept my voice as calm as I could. "Be strong."

"I'm trying. I wish I had your confidence, Michael."

"You guys can get through this. I know it. You're two of the toughest people I know. This is just one of life's challenges you have to get through. And I'll be here to help however I can."

"That means a lot, buddy. See you tomorrow. Bye."

My eyes filled as I sat there, not able to believe what I'd just heard, not sure I felt as confident as I'd made Nick believe. I thought about what I'd said to Nick about praying, and also about how I'd not done that too much lately, so I wasn't sure it would do any good.

I pulled the gearshift of my Jeep back to drive and stepped on the gas, not noticing the truck bearing down on me. I hit the brakes, closed my eyes, and tensed up. The sound of screeching brakes and blaring horn finally stopped after the truck swerved and rolled on past. I opened my eyes in time to see his hand out the window offering me one lone finger. Another deep breath, a good look behind me, and then I pulled onto the road.

I thought of going home but knew my mom's intuition would detect that I was upset before I even got my jacket off, so I just decided to go to Harry's by myself for a few beers.

As I pulled into the crowded lot, my headlights flashed across a young woman heading for the entrance. No way, I thought. It's Susan. I'd not seen her since Nashville and was not happy to see her now. She must have recognized my Jeep because she flashed me a fake smile and a quick wave as she hurried toward the front door. *Damn, she saw me, maybe I should just leave. But Jackie is probably in there or coming soon and Susan will tell her she saw me and I never came in, and that would just be a big mess.* And there was a part of me that wanted to see Jackie after my call with Nick.

Inside Harry's I purposely didn't scan the crowd as I made my way to the one unoccupied barstool next to the pool table, sat down and gave a nod to a short, stocky bartender headed my way.

"Hey, Jesse, how you doing? Looks like a good night."

Jesse smiled; his dark eyes glanced over my shoulder quickly. "Hey, Michael. Yeah, not sure what's going on tonight, but it seems like all the regulars are in, plus some people I don't think I've seen before. Anyhow, how are you? Miller Lite?"

"Yes, all good," I said, making my voice sound positive. "My plans are up in the air at the moment, so I decided to come stay with my mom for a little while and get reacquainted with the hometown."

Jesse placed the brown longneck in front of me. "Nick coming in tonight?"

I paused, "No, uh, no. He was going to, but something came up with his in-laws."

Jesse smiled as he turned to serve another patron, "Oh yeah, I remember those days."

I didn't really notice what was going on in the bar. My mind raced with all the potential outcomes of what Nick had just told me. I watched people shoot pool, guys trying to pick up girls, and a bachelor party getting way more drunk than they should. About a half hour later and on my second beer, I was hugged from behind. Truth be told, I smelled her before I felt the hug. I loved that smell.

I turned, looking into her deep brown eyes. "Hi, what's up?" She gave me a kiss.

"I was going to ask you the same question." Jackie smiled at the guy on the barstool next to me. "Hi. Can I just slide in here for a minute?" He nodded with a smile, as most men do when dealing with Jackie. I looked over and gave a nod of appreciation. He just kept smiling and gave me a thumbs up.

She sat on my lap as I reached for my beer and took a sip. I nodded to Jesse and pointed to the bottle and held up my index finger. "Well, I must say it's nice to see you back in Harry's, but why alone?" she asked. "I thought you were getting together with Nick." She thanked Jesse when the beer arrived, then turned back to me. "Everything OK? You don't look too happy. Is it because of the football thing?"

I just shook my head, and took a deep breath. "No it's not that. Nick called me on the way over." I paused, looking into those brown eyes. "Do me a favor, Jack, and don't let this go any further for now."

She tilted her head. "Sure, babe, sure."

"Nick told me Anna has cancer. They just found out."

She put her hand to her mouth. "Oh my God," she gasped.

Before I could respond, another voice came from behind me. "*Oh my God* what?"

It was Susan. She stumbled into me, spilling some of her clear drink on my shoulder. She draped an arm around Jackie, who I'm sure got the message I sent when I shook my head slightly.

"Hey girl, you look really great tonight," said Jackie. "Give me a minute and I'll be right over."

"OK," Susan slurred. "But what did you say 'Oh my God' about?"

"Oh, nothing big. Michael was just telling me about a friend of his mother's that I know who passed away." A guy walked behind Susan, bumping her gently. She turned and stumbled away with him.

Jackie looked back to me. "Sorry, she's just really kind of a lost soul right now. Ever since her dad died, she's just partying way too much." She paused and looked at Susan, now kissing the guy. "She means well."

"Do you really think so? I know we all get a little lost sometimes." I paused, taking another sip. "I'm feeling that way a bit myself, but with Susan I think it's more about her being a bitch. She's always been self-centered. And after her last escapade in Nashville, I just don't have any time for her anymore. It's tragic about her dad, but she's got to move on."

"Well, maybe, but come on, Michael. Her dad was killed on his way to her graduation from Clemson. Give her a break. With all due respect, you feeling lost because you just got cut from an NFL team after making a few million bucks these last few years does not compare at all with what Susan is dealing with." She paused, then finished in an irritated tone, "You'll forgive me if I'm not feeling too bad for you. But it's not about her right now, or you. Tell me about Anna."

I felt like a scolded child. "All I know at this point is that Anna found out this past week, and her parents and Nick's parents were coming over so she and Nick can tell them. I still can't believe it."

She leaned in and gave me a kiss on the cheek. "Michael, I know Anna and I have had our differences, but this makes me real sad. Is there anything I can do?"

I didn't answer right way. I scratched at the label on my beer bottle, recalling my many conversations with Anna about Jackie and me. Anna was the closest thing I had to a sister, and our talks usually happened after Jackie and I had a fight and I'd be trying to figure it out, to get an answer. Anna was always neutral, with no judgment. I asked her once if she liked Jackie, and if she thought Jackie was good for me. Anna said that if she responded, she'd be answering the question that only I could answer, and that would not be fair to me. I smiled at the memory.

Jackie brought me back from my thoughts. "What's the smile for?"

"Oh, I was just thinking about Anna and a talk we had."

"Yeah, I'll bet she had some things to say about me." She looked at me, her eyes filling just a bit. "Michael, it's very clear to me that Anna doesn't particularly care for me. She probably thinks I'm a spoiled brat and not a good match for you." She paused. "And I have my opinion of her as well, but I'm not going to get into it now. Regardless of our past, I'm sad about her having cancer."

We sat in silence for a moment, then she continued as she turned to me with sad eyes. "So? What about us? Is Anna right? Am I not a good match for you? For us?"

I took a deep breath and a swig of my beer. The guy next to us rose and said we could have his place. I guided Jackie from my lap to the barstool.

"Jack, seems there's a lot of. . . ." I paused. "Let's just call them differences where you and I are concerned. Shit, I knew what they were that night we first met at the beach party." I smiled softly, "Remember that night?"

Her sad eyes filled and she winked, taking my hand. "Yep, pretty sure I'll always remember that one."

"Yeah, me too. But I knew. Nick and I talked about it a lot. You were the pretty rich girl from the private school, whose dad was known about town to be an . . ." My voice trailed off.

"Ass," she filled in. "It is what it is. And you were the focused, responsible, handsome football star from a single-parent home, whose mom worked real hard to provide for you. We were certainly from different worlds."

"Yeah, we were. Guess we still are. It just seemed after that night we met, and even over the years of dating, we made those differences the focus of our relationship. I knew from the first time I met your dad he didn't like me, although I think he did like the idea of his daughter dating a Division 1 football player. That was probably a big reason you and I fought so much and did that on-again, off-again thing."

"Yep, Daddy sure isn't one to hide how he feels. But deep down he's a decent guy. He just needs to get better at showing it, and I do think he'd come to like you. . . ."

I interrupted, "Jack, it's OK. I get it. He's this super-successful guy. Strong, respected, wealthy, prominent, and I can see why he'd want the same for his daughters. Well, at least for you. Sometimes I'm not so sure he really even likes your sister."

"Oh, they can battle for sure. He loves Evie, but she's different in her approach, right?" She laughed. "I mean, I can remember the time Evie told Dad he should meditate; that he needed to chill out and get more in touch with his heart. That was a classic discussion." We both laughed a bit when Jackie said it was more likely her dad would pay money to *not* have to meditate.

"I'm pretty sure that being an unemployed ex-NFL player at age 27 doesn't qualify me as successful in your dad's eyes." I looked straight at her. "What about you? You got the answer about us yet?"

"No, not yet, I'm still trying to figure it out." She stood, placing her hands on my thighs and leaning in close to my face. "But what about Anna? Maybe I could send her some flowers, or have a restaurant in town send her and Nick some meals. Maybe pick a certain night of the week and send dinner. What do you think?"

"Flowers are always good, but I really have no idea what they need at the moment. Let me talk to Nick and Anna tomorrow and I'll let you know."

"OK." She took a sip of her beer, looking across the bar, then back to me. "I'd come with you—if that would even be OK—but I have an appointment I need to keep. I do, however, want to get together again soon. Sound good?"

I nodded, kissing her on the cheek before she walked away to visit with friends in a booth on the other side of the bar. I had one more beer, watched part of a college game, and talked with a few old friends that stopped by.

As I was getting ready to leave, a guy with a close-cropped beard and wearing a black baseball cap stopped at the empty stool next to me. His hair, showing traces of gray, hung below the hat, past his collar. He looked at me with intense aqua eyes. "OK to sit here?"

"Sure. I'm heading out, so this one will be open in a minute too."

"Thanks, but I'm good, just me. Have a nice night and be careful."

He ordered a Miller Lite. I paid my tab, shook hands with Jesse and decided to stop by to say goodbye to Jackie. I got up off the stool, turning toward the guy next to me. "Have a good one."

"Thanks, you too. Peace."

I was a few steps away when a feeling I cannot explain caused me to glance back over my shoulder at the guy, seeing him watching the game, his untouched beer still resting on the bar napkin in front of him.

CHAPTER 4

The Problem

*Let us run with perseverance the race that is
set before us. - Hebrews 12:1*

I opened my eyes the next morning, instantly aware of the softness of the sheets; *thread count* is what I've been told it is. I took a deep breath, pulling in the familiar fragrance of the blond streaked hair gently touching my nose. Jackie snuggled into me. She opened her eyes and looked into mine. No words, just a brief connection. I let out a deep breath, staring at the ceiling as my mind raced.

Damn, why did I come over last night? I should have gone right to my Jeep and gone home. Now what is this going to do to us? A rekindling? Another try? Or just a one-night hookup? Shit, shit, shit.

I grabbed my phone off the table: 7:11. *OK, I'll lie here for a few minutes, otherwise she'll be pissed if I just get up and leave.*

After about 10 minutes, I rolled over and kissed her forehead. "Gotta get going. I'll let you know what I find out about Anna."

She hugged me tight. "Want to get a shower before you leave?"

I shook my head. *That's the last thing I want right now.* "No, it's OK. You get some rest, I've got to get rolling, got a busy day."

She sat up, her eyes looking intently into mine. "Dinner tonight?"

"I don't know, Jack. I just don't know. I'll text you later."

She lay back down and rolled over as I got dressed. I walked downstairs and out the front door, taking in a deep breath of the cool autumn air. It felt good after the intense heat of training camp and preseason in Nashville. I stopped quickly and my jaw tensed as I saw a black Mercedes sedan pull into the parking spot not far from my Jeep. Jackie's dad looked at me as he got out of his car.

I strode down the walk to where he stood and extended my hand. "Hi, Mr. Jennings." He glared at my hand.

"Really?" he said. "Really?" He shook his head, then looked away and back to me. "Michael, I must thank that linebacker for the hit he put on you. I'm pretty sure that allowed me to win my bet on the spread. Sorry about your shortened career. I see you had no choice but to crawl back home." He smirked.

My slight smile seemed to irritate him as he stood up straight, a true alpha male with his workout shirt stretched tight across his broad chest and shoulders.

"And now this," he continued. "I stop by here early on my way to the gym to merely drop some mail off for my daughter. I wasn't even going to knock or go in. And this is what I see. Please tell me you just got here a few minutes ago to deliver a latte and a blueberry scone."

I shook my head slowly, still sporting my smirk. He took a step closer. "Come on, man. Haven't you figured this out yet? You need to move on. Stay away from Jackie, she's OK with it, trust me. You just have to stop coming around. What part don't you understand?"

"Oh, I understand fully. But just so you know, Jackie's been coming around a little, too. She made sure to visit Nashville."

"Yeah, well, it was probably to see you for the last time as a pro football player. Just stay away from her. Move on, son, and try to make something of yourself now. Maybe teaching, or maybe you could even get a high school coaching job." He glared at me, taking a deep breath. "Right?"

I stepped to the side as he walked by, then took a few steps looking toward my Jeep. "Yep, right." I paused, then uttered one last word just loud enough for him to hear. "Asshole."

"Hey, Michael." His voice was louder, forceful. I turned. "You don't want to go there." His stare lingered as I turned and jumped in my Jeep.

A few blocks away I pulled to the curb in front of Brew Ha Ha. A long line wound away from the counter. There were lots of baseball hats and headbands.

My time in line gave me a minute to process my meeting with Mr. Jennings. *Man, that guy is just so pissed. Why doesn't he like me? I mean, OK, I grew up middle class, but I worked hard. Damn, I got a full scholarship to a Division 1 school. I've always treated Jackie with respect, but I guess he doesn't see it that way. Oh well, I'll deal with that later.*

I grabbed my phone and texted Nick. His came back quickly:

Nick: Rough night, why don't you come over around lunchtime?

Me: I'll be there.

I tossed a $5 bill in the tip jar, thanked the girl who handed me my bagel and coffee, and headed toward the door. A man caught my eye, though he didn't see me. It was the guy with the long hair and slight beard I'd seen at Harry's last night. His black baseball cap fit in perfectly with the Saturday-morning crew in the shop. As I passed him, he was handing the metal cream container to a young woman with a baby on her hip.

"Thanks, she said. "Have a nice day."

"You too." He smiled at the baby, who extended his hand, pulling away from his mom and causing her to spill her hot coffee on her hand. She lost her balance and the toddler fell to the hardwood floor with a thud. I swear I heard a distinct *snap*. I turned and headed toward them, but ball cap guy was already there, reaching down as the toddler screamed. The child's arm looked like a small hockey stick. Ball cap guy wrapped both his hands on the arm for a second, then scooped the toddler up swiftly, placing him into the woman's open arms. The baby buried his face in his mother's shoulder as people scurried about offering assistance.

A minute later the toddler turned around and reached out the arm, a very straight arm, toward ball cap guy as his mom wiped tears and snot from his chubby little red face. Ball cap guy held the small hand and smiled back, then looked at the woman.

"Thank you so much," she said. "I thought he might have broken something."

"No," ball cap guy said. "He's gonna be fine, just one of many tumbles, right?" She nodded and gave a "you can say that again" look. "He's a tough little guy," ball cap guy added. "You two have a nice day. Peace." She smiled as he turned away.

I found myself not smiling at all. I'm sure my face bore a look of confusion as I held the door for an incoming older couple. Walking to the Jeep, I turned back a few times, looking for nothing in particular. *Man, that was weird. I could have sworn that snap was a breaking bone, maybe not as loud as the many I've heard over my football years, but it was the same sound. And the angle of that little guy's arm . . . it was messed up. I know what I saw. And then that guy handed him back to his mom . . . and it was fine.*

I took a deep breath. *Maybe all the stress is getting to me.* I got in the Jeep and drove to my mom's house.

Mom was at the kitchen table with a cup of tea when I came in. She smiled as I leaned in and kissed her head. She was in workout gear, having come back from a run, and her shoulder-length hair was pulled back in a ponytail. Mom looked great, and I marveled at how she was always put together as she approached her 50th birthday. I'd asked her recently how she felt with 50 just around the corner. "It's only a number, honey . . . only a number." Since she had married early and had me at 22-years-old, we were closer in age than many of my friends and their moms. "She looks more like your sister than your mom" is a comment I've heard many times.

"Nice run?" I asked, sitting at the table and taking my bagel from the bag.

"Really good. The air is just the right temperature—not too cold yet." She took a sip of tea, peering over the rim of the mug. "Thanks for the text last night that you were staying at Jackie's. I can't say I was jumping for joy, but I do appreciate you letting me know. I'm glad you're staying with me until you get clear on what comes next."

I pulled out the chair and sat down with my coffee. "Me too, Mom. And thanks for not lecturing or getting mad."

She smiled, dramatically biting her lip. "Oh, come on now, you're too old to lecture. Even if I wanted to." She laughed. "Michael, you know I like Jackie, she's a nice girl. I know she and I think differently on some things, and that's OK, I guess." She wrapped both hands around her mug, moving it in small circles on the table. "I'm sure things will work out, whatever you do."

"Thanks, Mom." I put my hand on hers. "I do have some bad news I want to tell you. Not sure how to say it . . . so I'll just say it. Nick didn't meet me last night because both their parents were coming over." I paused.

"Michael, what is it?"

"Mom, Anna has cancer."

She looked at me for a moment before putting her hands together, as if in prayer, and placing them over her lips.

"Oh, no. I cannot believe it. And just after getting married this past spring." She shook her head. "What kind is it? Does she have treatment lined up? Is it curable?"

"Mom, Mom, slow down. I just found out last night and am going to head over to see Anna and Nick shortly. I'll let you know what I find out, but right now I just wanted to tell you." I finished my bagel as we continued to discuss Anna's situation, then I stood, and so did my mom.

She gave me a kiss on the cheek, and then a hug, whispering into my ear, "You've always been a good friend to Nick, and I'm sure he's going to need a lot of support now. Be patient with him."

I pulled away. "That's my plan, Mom. Guess we're both gonna need each other now."

I showered then made the drive to Nick and Anna's place. Her parents' car was parked out front along with another car I didn't recognize.

Nick was at the door as I approached. His eyes were a little red, but he was clean-shaven, wearing jeans and a pressed shirt. He looked a little heavier than when we'd last seen each other. He smiled as we embraced. "Thanks for coming over."

"Sure, I wanted to see you guys." A strong aroma of coffee hung in the air, and I saw the familiar green-and-white bags from Tornetta's bakery on the counter. Anna rose from where she sat next to her mom and dad and her best friend, Sheila. She took the bunch of sunflowers I extended for her and smiled. I searched her face and body for any trace of her sickness, and found nothing. She looked beautiful in jeans and a camel-colored sweater.

"Thanks, Michael. I love the sunflowers. Thanks so much for coming over." Her green eyes sparkled beneath the brown bangs of her long hair, and her smile was one that had always made me feel real good.

Anna had always been a hugger. The first time we met, we were all seniors in college. She'd come home with Nick, and one thing I remember is all the hugs she gave people; people she was meeting for the first time. Anna had a great NCAA career, competing in the 400- and 800-meter races, as well as being an Academic All-American in the high jump, throwing her 5-foot-9-inch frame to school-record heights.

Yes, Anna was a hugger for sure, but something about this one was different from the hundreds that had come before. I was ready to pull away, but she continued hugging. Then, as we did, I looked at her. "I'm really sorry, Anna. This should not be happening."

Anna's mom and dad got up and we exchanged greetings. Both had gray hair and looked older than the last time I'd seen them at the wedding. Anna was their youngest.

I gave Sheila a hug, too. Nick handed me a mug of steaming coffee and a plate holding a cannoli and biscotti. I always loved it when Anna's parents came, and the baked goods they'd bring that satisfied my sweet tooth, although today the food didn't tempt me.

"My mom wanted me to make sure and tell you she sends her love, and you know she'll be praying for you."

"Thanks, Nick," said Anna's mom. "Please tell your mom we appreciate it, and keep the prayers coming. We just need to heed the words of St. Francis de Sales, 'God will protect us or give us the unfailing strength to bear it.' "

"Yes, lots of strength is gonna be needed for sure, Mrs. Russo." I nodded. "And I'll be sure to tell my mom you said hello."

I sat at the table as Nick glanced at Anna, who nodded slightly. He looked to me. "Some news, huh?" He paused. "So, what we know, Michael, is that Anna has non-Hodgkin lymphoma, or NHL as it's called. It's a cancer. . . ." Nick stopped and began to tear up as Anna reached for his hand. He looked at her as she wiped the tears from his face. Anna's mom rubbed the silver cross hanging around her neck. Her dad just sat with his elbows on his knees, his chin resting on his hands.

Nick continued. "It begins in the lymph nodes, and that's how Anna found it. She found some lumps in her neck and went to the doctor. Her doctor's a great lady and said it was good she came in right away. As you know, getting this early is always a good thing." He paused, shaking his head. "It's just hard for me to use those words, 'a good thing,' when I'm talking about this."

I glanced at Anna's parents: her mom's fingers still on cross, dad's chin still on his hands.

"Yeah. It just doesn't seem fair. I'm really sorry about this. What did the doctor say about treatment? What's gonna happen now?"

Anna sat up, and took a deep breath. "Well, she said this is definitely a curable type of cancer and it's"—she leaned over to kiss Nick on the cheek—"a good thing that I'm young and strong." Nick smiled.

"I'm sure that will make a difference," I confirmed.

"Yes, it will. Although, because this type of cancer can disrupt and weaken my immune system, I'm going to have to be real careful and get lots of rest." She shrugged. "And working out won't be such a big priority now. I don't see this as fair or not; it's just something that's happening in my life—in all our lives right now.

"Dr. Chelson—that's my doctor's name—said she's got some more work to do. We have an appointment in a few days where she'll recommend treatment. She said it will likely be chemo, probably beginning soon." She took a deep breath and looked to the others in the room. "And if that's the case, I'm going to get tired and need a lot of support, and—" she smiled, running her hand through her hair—"probably go with the bald look for a while."

Silence hung for a moment, until Anna rose and went to her dad and kissed his balding head. "But I'm guessing I've got a nice round head like yours under this hair, so it will be OK." He laughed nervously, wrapping his arms around her waist.

"Yeah, honey. Yeah, it will all be fine. You're a strong one." He wiped away his tears.

"You all know that I'll help in whatever way I can," I said.

Anna smiled slightly. "Thank you, Michael. I'm trusting in that. And I'm glad Nick has you as a friend. He's gonna need you."

Anna's mom invited us all into the kitchen for more pastries and coffee, as I settled in next to Sheila. We'd first met a few years earlier at dinner when Anna and Nick were playing Cupid and doing their best to get us together. I remembered how excited Anna was when she told me about Sheila and the work she did as a nurse at the children's hospital a few towns over.

"Hey, Sheila, how you doing?"

"Hi, Michael, probably feeling just like you."

"I know all the stuff about her being young and catching it early, but it just sucks."

She shook her head. "I just don't get a lot of the time how this happens to such good, nice people. I see way too much of it at work, and I just question it."

"I've been thinking the same thing. Not sure how God can let stuff like this happen to people like Anna and Nick."

She took off her baseball cap, ran her fingers through her long red hair, and replaced the cap. "Yes indeed, would love to meet him in person for a quick talk about that. In fact, I have to leave for my yoga class soon. There's actually a cool guy in the class I'm going to talk to about this very subject."

She crossed one foot in front of the other as she leaned against the counter. "I'm glad that you're here, Michael. It's nice to have you home again, especially with this news. Sorry to hear about you getting let go in Nashville. Your mom said you got some tryouts but no offers. That must be tough."

"Thanks, Sheila, I guess my problems aren't such a big deal next to what Anna's facing." She nodded. "I've got a lead about playing in Canada, but that wouldn't start until spring. In the meantime, I'm exploring some options around here to keep me busy over the winter."

"That's great. I'm sure things will work out on the career front." She paused, looking down at her sneakers, then back to me. "And how's Jackie?"

The look on my face during my slow-to-respond pause let Sheila know I had not been expecting that. "Uh, uh, she's OK. I guess."

"Michael, you're a nice, good-looking guy, and I'm glad we've become friends through Anna and Nick. You should be proud of your time playing football in the pros, and now in this next phase of your journey. . . ." She paused, leaning in to give me a kiss. "You'll figure it out. And who knows, maybe we'll even go on another date." She winked as she turned.

After Sheila left, I hung out in the kitchen for about an hour. Anna's parents said they had to get going but would be back for dinner. We said our goodbyes, and I ducked into the bathroom before getting ready to leave. As I was coming out, I heard Anna and Nick talking in the kitchen.

"It was good to see my parents; I'm glad they came over. And it will be good to see yours again tomorrow."

I heard Nick's voice. "Yes, it was. They seem like they're taking it OK . . . or as best as can be expected." He paused, then continued in a lower voice that I could barely hear. "Should we tell them the rest?"

"No, not yet. I'm not ready. You can tell Michael—but only him— if you need to talk to someone besides me."

I retreated to the bathroom, then stomped down the hall and made a loud sound with the door before walking into the kitchen. Part of me wanted so bad to say "Tell Michael what?" but the feeling in my gut discouraged it.

"Hey, Michael, before you go, I wanted to ask how things have been going with you," said Nick. He looked at Anna. "We've been kinda self-centered here all night."

"No problem, guys," I said quickly. "To answer your question, I'm staying with my mom for a while until I figure things out. I have a chance at playing in the CFL next season, so I've got to stay fit over the winter. I worked hard to get where I am, and I don't think I'm ready to give up on that dream yet. But hey, I don't want you to spend any time thinking about me. Everything is going to work out for me . . . just as it will for you. And whatever you need, just ask me."

"Thanks, Michael," said Nick.

I could see that Anna was tired, so I pulled out my car keys. "OK, you guys, I'm gonna get going too."

I looked at them as the three of us hugged. "I love you both very much and am praying this will all be OK—that you'll soon be in remission, Anna." Tears rolled down my face. "I need you both around for a long, long time." Tears now streamed down on all our faces. I gave them each a kiss and headed out the door, then took a very, very deep breath.

CHAPTER 5

The Thoughts

As he thinketh in his heart, so is he.
- Proverbs 23:7

As my mom and I walked into St. John's on Sunday morning, I took her arm and she smiled. The little bit of gray in her hair highlighted the brown that fell to her shoulders. She was wearing gray wool slacks with a white turtleneck and a navy wrap around her shoulders. My mom would often say to me, "Michael, all I need are you, some great friends, and a wonderful stylist to do my color, and everything will be OK." I always loved the smile and laugh that accompanied that comment. My mom was one of those . . . gotta be careful how I say this . . . maturing women who look great with long, straight hair. Her green eyes were my favorite thing about Mom. It seemed there was nothing I couldn't get through when she looked at me with those eyes and told me she loved me.

We settled into a pew as Mom waved to some of her friends; I smiled and waved too. I knelt to attempt a few prayers, then sat back. I felt arms coming around my neck as I did. It was my mom's best friend, Cathy. "Hello, Michael, nice to see you here with your mother. You get more handsome every time I see you."

I smiled and turned, kissing her on the cheek. "Hi, Aunt Cathy, nice to see you." I turned and stood as the music began; it was one of my favorites, *Here I Am, Lord*. I'd not heard it in a long time. *I guess you won't hear hymns when you don't go to church.*

I was happy to see Father Green, a younger priest and one I'd enjoyed hearing preach in the past, walking up the aisle. A young altar server held the crucifix straight and smiled my way; I smiled back, giving the thumbs up sign. I was pretty sure her dad was the man a few pews ahead of me holding up his iPhone with the intensity of Martin Scorsese.

Father Green's warm and easy style pulled at my attention. His voice was conversational and his face always held a welcoming look. I let thoughts of Jackie, my next career move, and the pending challenge for Anna float to the back of my mind and focused on listening. One part of the readings that really got my attention were these words of St. Paul: "I have fought the good fight, I have finished the race, I have kept the faith."

Father Green really made sense of the Gospel message and seemed to understand the challenges we all face in life. He spoke simply, offering us things to consider in our lives instead of telling us what we needed to do. He recalled the life of Job, a wealthy man who lost everything in a test to see if he would continue to worship God. It was as if the message was customized for the recent events in my life, and my state of doubt and confusion. I was glad I'd come with Mom that morning, even though my recent attendance at Mass had been spotty.

I leaned over to Mom during his homily. "This guy sure is easy to listen to. He gets me thinking." Right after the final blessing, she whispered in my ear, "We should ask Father Green if he'd like to grab a cup of coffee or lunch." I nodded.

People were gathered around Father Green in the back of the church like a quarterback after a victory, and as we approached he was down on one knee by two youngsters being shown all the karate moves of their toy spaceman. I spoke with Mom and Aunt Cathy as we waited for the crowd to disperse.

"Well, hello, Sharon and Cathy, how are you two?" Father Green hugged both women.

"Hi, Father, we're doing great," my mom said. She looked at me. "And I think you've met my son, Michael."

I smiled, extending my hand. "Hi, Father, nice to see you again."

"You too, Michael. You're a lucky man to be with these two wonderful ladies. Nice to have you back in town. Sorry about things not working out in Nashville, but I'm glad to see you're looking strong and healthy after that hit."

"Thanks, Father. Yep, I'm doing OK. And as for these two, trust me, Father, they remind me all the time how lucky I am to know them!" Laughter echoed off the stone walls. After a few minutes of conversation, Aunt Cathy said her goodbye.

"Father," my mom said, "Michael and I thought if you had nothing scheduled this afternoon, we'd love to buy you lunch. Any interest?"

"Sure, great idea. I need to do some work cleaning up in the rectory garden, but I can do that later after lunch. How about I meet you at O'Leary's Pub in about 15 minutes?"

Mom and I looked at each other in agreement. Father Green made his way up the aisle and disappeared behind the altar and into the sacristy. As we moved toward the door, I said, "Mom, just give me a minute over here." I made my way to the statue of St. Joseph, Jesus' earthly father and an inspiration for many fathers, and knelt down. My own father had left my mom and me when I was seven, and my relationship with him was not good. But I'd always had an attraction to St. Joseph. Over the years I'd asked him for help and guidance, but as I knelt there, I couldn't think of the last time I had. I closed my eyes and began:

> *St. Joseph. Just stopping here a moment to ask for*
> *some help for me and some friends. I'm feeling mixed up*

*for sure about a lot in life now. It just seems hard, and
unfair. I'm not sure what to do about Jackie, and it seems
to be on my mind all the time. And my present employ-
ment situation sucks, oh, sorry, I mean it stinks. So if you
will, please help me out with these, let me get some type
of answer, some direction to take. But most of all I pray
you keep an eye on my friend Anna who just found out
she has cancer. Please protect her and let the treatment
work for her so she again can get back to being a healthy
young lady. And keep her husband, my friend Nick, on
your watch as well. He's a strong guy, but this may test
him. Thanks, St. Joseph. Amen.*

A few minutes later, Mom and I settled into a booth at O'Leary's.
It had a warm feeling, fueled in part by flaming logs in the stone fire-
place on the far wall. The smell of the burning wood reminded me of
the fires Mom and I had made together so many times on Christmas
morning.

Father Green joined us, removing his jacket and placing it on the
bench next to him. "Thanks so much for this invite to lunch, you two."

Mom answered, "Oh, Father, it's our pleasure. Michael and I like
when you say Mass. We were talking this morning about how you have
this way of simplifying the message in your homily."

I nodded. "Yes, it sure was that way today. I'm really glad I came to
Mass, Father." I took a sip of my water.

Father Green smiled. "Me too. And Sharon and Michael, I'd like
you to call me Matt." He paused. "If that's OK with you."

"Oh, Father, I'm not sure," my mom said.

Father Green looked at me then tilted his head in my mom's
direction. I got the hint. "Mom, come on, it's OK," I said. "I think we'll
be fine calling him Matt. Let's give it a try, and I'll keep an eye out for
any lightning bolts." We all had a good laugh.

The waiter came and took our order, all three of us going with sandwiches and fries.

"So, Michael, what was it in today's message that got your attention?" Matt asked as he fiddled with his spoon.

I took a deep breath. "Good question, Matt. The main thing, I think, is our need to know that sometimes"—I paused—"many times, there are people suffering, and it just doesn't make any sense to us, kind of like Job. We just learned that my best friend's wife was diagnosed with cancer. They were just married this past year. Ever since I heard the news, I can't understand it. I mean, why?" I shook my head.

Matt paused. "Yeah, that's a tough one. What's her name?"

"Anna."

"How's Anna doing with it?" he asked, his eyes intently on mine.

"It's weird to me, but she doesn't seem as panicked as I'd be in her shoes. I'm glad I can be here to go through this with them." I paused. "And I guess it helps that her mom and dad are very religious people and have a strong support network."

Our sandwiches arrived, and Matt led us in a simple grace.

"Matt, what really got me today and what I struggle with is the notion of 'running the race,' as you discussed today. I've heard that many times over the years and have always attributed it to St. Paul." I took a bite and watched the waiters moving quickly in the pub. "I guess right now, Anna's race is just really hard to run. Mine, too. I feel really lost at the moment. And I'm tired. Just very tired, like I lost a part of myself. I used to have so much energy for my job—for football—and my life. And now I'm not sure I can help myself, let alone support Nick and Anna."

He nodded. "I get it. And you know, Sharon and Michael, that I too feel that way often. Sometimes it's because I'm tired or suffering, or people I love are suffering. Not a week goes by when someone doesn't come to me with a very similar situation to yours. Only two weeks ago a couple came to me to talk about the loss of their teenage son."

Mom shook her head. "And what did you tell them?"

Matt smiled compassionately. "Nothing."

Mom and I sat still, until she spoke. "Nothing?"

"Well, I can see your confusion. And tell is the key word here. I've found over the years that my role is to support them, perhaps lead them a bit to get or gain some strength, and to trust that God does love them, and he's not abandoned them." He emphasized the word "trust."

"OK, I am confused. You don't tell them anything?" I asked.

"No. I merely listen. And ask questions."

"Questions? Like what?" Mom listened as Matt and I talked.

"Well, there's no set textbook method. It sort of depends on the situation and the person. But mostly, I'll look to move the person to understanding that God is not the man behind the curtain—like in *The Wizard of Oz*—pulling the strings and making all this stuff happen in life. Our world is not perfect; it unfolds from that place of imperfection. Sometimes it's easy and good, and sometimes not. But one thing for sure is that it is not perfect—it was never intended to be."

"Hmmm, that's for sure. I guess it's like what Anna's mom said about God either protecting us or giving us the strength to bear it."

Matt nodded. "Yes. That's a great insight from St. Francis de Sales. He has many writings with this theme." He took the final bite of sandwich and placed his napkin on the plate. "That's a strong way to think for many people. And the other way I've heard people describe suffering is that everything happens for a reason."

"Oh yeah, I've heard that one before. Do you really believe that?"

"It's true, if that's what someone believes. Then the question and work for them is to determine what the reason is. What can they learn from it? How can they evolve? Continue to change and grow? I've talked with many people who hold that philosophy. But. . . ." He paused, then finished his thought. "God is not the cause of what happened. We must remember that while God can control this world and our lives, He doesn't. Things take place in this world as they do . . . because of nature or because of people, and their free will to choose. God is not up there behind the curtain pulling the strings."

"You know Father"—Mom stopped, then looked at me—"and Matt. I've come to adopt that philosophy. When my husband, Michael's father, left us, I was always looking at myself wondering what I could have done differently. Did I pay enough attention to him? Was I pretty enough? Social enough? Smart enough? I guess I blamed myself. And it was exhausting.

"Over time, and after many, many conversations with people, I started looking at it a different way, started thinking what I could learn from the experience and how I could use it to make me better."

Matt smiled and put his hand across the table on my mom's for a few seconds. "And this way of moving through your husband's departure has served you well, Sharon. God did not make your husband leave; he made the choice to leave. And you made the choice to not let the experience destroy you or your faith. That makes you one strong woman."

"Thank you, Father. I've worked hard to reach that point of understanding."

Matt turned to me. "Does Anna believe in something bigger than us?"

I shifted in the booth. "You mean God?"

"I guess, but maybe not. When you said earlier that Anna's parents are religious people, I wondered if Anna is too. You see, my belief is in God, as our faith describes it. But for others, it may be different. Religion is just the formal structure of one's beliefs."

I nodded. "I see. So yes, I'd say Anna believes in something bigger that she calls God."

"This is good. So, some questions I'd likely ask are around how she views God. Is he some type of power or consciousness that's outside of her? I'd want Anna to get clear on the relationship she has with God."

I fiddled with my spoon, keeping my eyes on Matt. "Keep going."

"There's a guy I know who had an accident years ago that sent thousands of volts of electricity into him and a friend. The ladder they were lowering hit a high-tension line. He and his friend both died, but this guy came back. When he describes what happened, he gets to the point where his body stopped living, if you will, but a part of him kept going."

I looked at Mom, whose teary eyes never left Matt, her brow creased. Matt went on. "He then describes being joined with a consciousness, in a very loving place, and communicating with this presence that he calls God. At one point, he expressed his love and concern for his mom and girlfriend and alludes that his passing will devastate them. It was in that cosmic instance that his spirit, his energy, his soul reentered his body, and he came back to life in this realm."

Mom and I sat quietly. I spoke, shaking my head. "Wow. Just . . . wow."

"Yes, wow indeed," said Matt. "You should meet my friend sometime."

"That would be cool. Maybe Anna would like it, too."

"Maybe," Matt continued. "But here's the key thing. You can be a friend and source of comfort to Anna by supporting her in whatever she believes. My friend believes that God is within him, and that that was the energy that left when he died and then reentered his body. So right now on his spiritual journey, he doesn't believe in praying to God as an external force."

Matt paused, taking a sip of water. "Then what?" I inquired.

Matt leaned in. "He believes in connecting with God as our internal energy of love."

"Hmm," I pondered. "And what do you think about that?"

A smile spread on Matt's face. "God is both. I believe differently than my friend in that I know God exists"—he raised his hand—"out here . . . whether my friend chooses to pray to him or not. And God is certainly within us all." He paused, glancing to my mom and then back to me. "And strengthening that connection—joining in the unity of love with God—well, that's really our life's work. I'd support Anna in both praying to God as she understands Him, and being sure to create times of stillness where she can join with the presence of the Spirit within her."

We finished our lunch. Mom insisted on paying, and Matt and I agreed that we needed to do this more often so that we could each have our turn picking up the check.

As we exited the pub, Matt and I hugged. He looked at me. "Listen, Michael. I'd be glad to talk with Anna and Nick, if either of them wants to. Or you can talk with them about it . . . or not, your call. Either way, I've got her on my list." He winked.

"Yeah," I smiled. "Thanks, Matt." He hugged my mom and we made our way to the parking lot.

CHAPTER 6

The Stranger

Be open to where it all may lead.

Mom and I stopped by the grocery store then headed home. She was driving and made a slight detour to go past the house we'd looked at, slowing down as we passed it. "You know, Michael, Mary said this is priced high and the seller is standing firm. She said it will probably be on the market for a while."

I leaned toward her, looking past her to the house. "OK, Mom, got it. It's just not gonna happen." She frowned and began driving again.

I stared out the passenger window, lost in thought.

"So what are you thinking about?" she asked.

"Oh, just stuff." I turned to her. "Like what Matt's friend said about God being in us, and not really about praying to an outside God, but rather connecting with His internal force that's with us. It's a different way of thinking about it for me. You raised me to believe in God, and I do."

Mom said, "Well, that's good. At least I can feel that Catholic school tuition was worth it." She laughed, smacking my shoulder. "There are a lot of my friends' kids who went to Catholic school and no longer practice the faith, and it really upsets them."

She stopped the car at a red light, and turned to me, lowering her Ray-Bans so I could see her eyes. "Michael, here's what I believe. There is a God; a wonderful loving energy that exists regardless of who chooses to believe or practice a faith founded on Christian principles.

God just is. And," she continued, "God is within all of us, and the more we can make that connection, as Father Green said, that union, well, my dear son, that's what it's all about." Her eyes were misty as she pointed her index finger at me and then used it to push up her sunglasses. The light turned green, but before accelerating she looked back to me. "This I know." We drove for a few blocks in silence.

I picked up the conversation. "I have a number of friends who have stopped going to church. They tell me they still believe in something bigger, but they've just moved away from the structure of their faith . . . like Matt said. I always thought of God as something external, like in all the prayers I learned to recite, that were directed at a loving and powerful God that was outside of us. But the stuff Matt talked about made sense, too. So now I'm confused. I may need to rethink my relationship with God."

The car came to a stop at yet another well-timed red light. I looked to my mom, who was staring at me. I smiled at the serendipity of my comment and the red light and wondered if Mom had some Yoda-Jedi-like power over traffic signals. Her lips were closed, her eyes a bit squinted.

I'd seen that look before, many times. "Mom, Mom, it's OK. Don't worry. I think this talk with Matt and the thinking I'm doing is a good thing. I'm not heading off to find any new churches, or the 'church of what's happening now' . . . as you call them. My belief is intact." I leaned over and kissed her cheek. "Everything just feels so unsettled at the moment."

"Yes, I understand, Michael. But lately I realized I used to be judgmental of people with different faiths and beliefs than mine. I've come to know so many beautiful and loving people who don't go to the same church as us that I'm more open to other interpretations of God and faith." She paused, shooting me a quick wink. "Maybe I'm just maturing. I'm glad your belief is strong—and don't worry too much, dear, it's all going to be OK."

"Yeah, I really hope so." A part of me wasn't sure about my mom's last statement as I stared at the passing homes just a few blocks from where I'd grown up. The emptiness that had been growing inside me rumbled.

I did a full workout, then decided to head over to Harry's. After all, it was Sunday and the NFL season was in full swing. I hadn't wanted to watch any games after leaving Nashville but decided it was time to get back in the game, since it was possible I'd either be playing in Canada or doing commentary. Not just *possible*; I was determined to make something happen.

If I hustled, I could make the late game.

Harry's had the most TV screens of any bar in town, each tuned to a different game. There was always a mix of fans. As expected, the place was crowded. Most people were decked out in jerseys, hats, and/ or t-shirts sporting their favorite team's logos and colors. I smiled at the dominance of the Eagles logo. I felt a bit out of place in my logo-less navy sweater and jeans; but then again, I really didn't know who I'd cheer for now. I shook my head as I considered the teams I'd played with the past few years. *I'm certainly not wearing any of their stuff.*

The outside deck was still open, as the day was cool and sunny but not cold, and I waved to some friends as I made my way up the ramp to the door. I wasn't in the mood to talk. I just wanted to have a few beers and watch a little football.

It looked like the early crowd had gone home, and there were a few empty seats, including a stool near the end of the bar. As I approached it, I noticed the cap of the man on the next stool. It was black, with white and gold letters across the front naming the team from New Orleans. Not a common cap in Pennsylvania. As I sat down on the stool, I realized the face under the cap belonged to the ball cap man I'd seen here a few nights earlier and at the coffee shop the day before that. A half-full glass of water sat on the coaster in front of him.

"This seat open?" I asked him.

"It's all yours," he said.

I smiled as I took the seat and said, "How's it going?" He turned, smiled and tipped his hat.

"Always good on Sundays this time of year. Of course, they're all good. A day of rest, right?"

Jesse walked up to me, extend his hand, and set a Miller Lite in front of me. "Hey, man, how are you? And how's Anna and Nick? Shitty news."

"Yeah, hey, Jesse. Thanks for asking. They're good. . . . Wait, how'd you find out?"

Jesse nodded toward the other side of the bar. I glanced over his shoulder to see a group of young men, clad in hats and jerseys from various teams. There in the middle, sitting on the lap of a guy in a Dallas Cowboys jersey, was Jackie's friend Susan.

"Oh, man, guess the word's out now. Shit." I took a swig of my beer.

"Sorry if I'm not supposed to know."

"No, don't worry, Jesse, not your fault. Nick said he figured it would spread fast, kind of always does with bad news." I looked across the bar at Susan, then back to Jesse. "Not sure it moves as fast with good news, though. Wonder why that is."

"Yeah, I agree. When you see them, please let them know I've got them in my prayers." Not sure why I thought about how Jesse prayed, and to whom, but I did, as he turned to the guy next to me.

"How you doing, Jay? Want that beer yet?'

"Not yet, Jesse, thanks. I'm good. I'll get it in a bit."

I watched the closest TV hanging behind the bar as the quarterback for the Saints, wearing number 9 on his jersey, jogged confidently to the huddle to call the first play of the game. His opponents from New York stood ready in their white and green uniforms. I turned, extending my hand. "Hey, Jay, we've not met officially yet, although we did talk in here a few nights ago, and I saw you at Brew Ha Ha yesterday. I'm Michael."

Jay took my hand and we shook. "Hi, Michael, nice to meet you. I remember you from the other night, but must have missed you at the coffee shop."

"Yeah, you were busy. I was there when that toddler fell and you picked him up and gave him back to his mom." I was studying Jay closely, and he looked back at me just as intently, his eyes the most unique shade of blue I've ever seen. "I thought for sure I heard a bone snap in that little guy, and that his arm was broken. It sure looked pretty crooked when I first saw it. But then you picked him up and he was fine. Very weird."

Jay rubbed his hands together lightly as they rested on the bar next to his water, a bracelet of brown and turquoise beads around his right wrist. "I thought that too, but seemed like he was OK. Just needed a little love to make the tears stop." He turned to me. "Children sure are resilient . . . in so many ways; wonder what happens to that as we get older."

I laughed. "Yeah, you can say that again. Resiliency is certainly a rare commodity with a lot of older people I know." Jay nodded, turning his gaze back to the TV just in time to see the All-Pro quarterback for the Saints throw a perfect pass that was caught in stride by his teammate at the 10-yard line and was in the end zone in another two strides.

"Yah!" Jay let out, joining the noise from patrons following the game. "I'm telling you, I think this could be a really good year." He turned to me. "Maybe even an NFC Championship or Super Bowl."

"So I'm guessing you're a Saints fan? You from New Orleans?"

"Oh, yes, how can you not like a team with a name like Saints?" He smiled and high-fived a guy in a Saints jersey walking by us. "I'm from a small town a few hours north of here. My dad was an Eagles fan, so I grew up watching them a lot but have just come to like the Saints—especially their quarterback—these past 10 years or so. He just seems to be such a good dude, and great leader."

I nodded, taking a sip of beer. "He sure is that, no question."

"How about you? Got a favorite team?"

I shook my head. "Not really."

"Well, from the size of you, it looks like you may have played some ball yourself. Heck, you look like you could even hang with these guys." Jay nodded toward the bank of TVs behind the bar.

I stared at the players on the screen for a few seconds, then turned to Jay. "Yeah, I played high school and college ball." I paused, then decided not to get into my recent past with a guy I hardly knew.

Jay moved his water glass as the other bartender placed a plate of wings in front of him. He thanked her, then grabbed a wing and took a bite. "Wing?" he asked, looking at me. I shook my head no. As a commercial came on the TV, he turned back to me. "What have you been doing since college?"

"Nothing much. Held a few jobs and moved around a bit. I grew up here and came back into town recently. My mom and some good friends are here, so I recently decided to settle down back here for a while." I changed the subject, hoping he wouldn't notice. "That offer of a wing still open?"

Jay nodded and placed a few on a plate and slid them my way, and I thanked him. He licked some sauce off his thumb, and nodded. "My pleasure." Jay and I talked off and on for the remainder of the game and even high-fived a few times when the Saints scored. We discussed who was the best running back of all time; I went with Barry Sanders while Jay passionately campaigned for Walter Payton—both on the field and off. We agreed on Montana for quarterback, while reluctantly acknowledging Brady and his career.

Jay ordered a Miller Lite just before halftime, then followed it up with another glass of water.

During the third quarter, I let it slip that I knew some of the players personally, and ended up telling Jay the story of my too-short NFL career. He listened sympathetically and asked just the right questions to get me talking about my frustrations and my current search for a direction in life, and my uncertainty about my relationship with Jackie. The only topic I didn't mention was Anna's cancer. That was still too raw. Even so, before I knew it the game was over and the Saints had rolled over their opponents by three touchdowns.

"You sure I can't buy you another beer? After all, I ate half your wings. And talked your ear off. I don't normally do either of those things with a stranger!"

Jay laughed, then stood and patted his belly. "Nope, gotta watch myself as I get older. I'm gonna walk home before it gets dark and maybe watch the Sunday night game. And I don't think we're strangers anymore, right? I enjoyed our conversation very much." He pulled some money off the bar, then slid a $10 bill to the edge for Jesse as he stopped in front of us. "Thanks, Jesse. See you again soon. Have a great week." He turned to me. "And I'm sure everything will work out for your friends, even with the new development."

That took me by surprise. I hadn't mentioned Anna and Nick to him. And what was the new development he was talking about? But

I was too shocked to say anything coherent. "Uh, sure. You got it, Jay. Have a good week yourself."

The loud sound of crashing glass interrupted our goodbye, as everyone in the bar turned to see a muscular guy being held by two others as he struggled to break free. Another man, wearing a T-shirt with *Exit Zero* across the front, stood alert in front of him, hands raised. Shouts of obscenities filled the corner near the pool table. Jesse was quickly over the bar. He talked with the involved parties, and they seemed to part ways, although the muscular guy continued to eye the *Exit Zero* guy.

"I'm not so sure that's over just yet," I said to Jay. "Crazy, huh?"

Jay placed his hand on my shoulder. "Nice to watch the game with you, Michael, and all the best with your transition back here to your home. I'm sure your mom is glad to have you here." He turned to go, then looked back at me and nodded toward the fighters. "And as for those guys, it'll be OK. That big guy is just too much up in his head; he'll drop down into his heart and it will be OK."

What an odd thing to say, I thought. My mouth was open as Jay walked directly toward the muscular dude, who was now standing ready like a soldier, a pool cue his weapon of choice. Jay placed his hand briefly on the guy's shoulder as he made his way through the crowd. I couldn't be sure, but he might have whispered a few words. The guy turned quickly, fists raised, then just followed Jay with his stare. He shook his head as if to clear it.

A few minutes later, it was me shaking my head as the muscular dude walked to the *Exit Zero* guy and leaned in to say a few words. The two shook hands, and muscular dude headed back to his group. The storm had passed.

I watched the pregame show for the evening game, then decided I'd head home. As I spoke with Jesse on my way out, I saw Susan stumble along the bar and out the door as some guy seemed to be arguing with her. Not much later I stepped into the fading daylight of the parking lot and noticed a group standing off to one side. As I got closer, I saw a woman sitting on the ground holding a rag to her bloody head. It was Susan.

Two policemen stood in the crowd next to the guy Susan had left the bar with. I'd seen him a few times before, and stopped next to him as he ran his hands through his hair. "Everything OK? She hurt bad?" I asked him.

"No, thank God. But she's got a good gash and gonna need some stitches." He looked at her, shaking his head.

"What happened?"

"Not sure. I was trying to get her to give me her keys, and we were gonna grab an Uber. You know her?"

I nodded, raising my brows. "I sure do."

The guy continued. "She was being a b—, she was being Susan. So I gave up and was headed back into the bar to find someone she knows better who might be able to help. Next thing I know, I hear a scream, and she's down."

"So . . . so, she just fell?"

"I guess, but the weird thing is she fell backward. Just can't understand that, since she was walking toward her car—or more like stumbling toward her car."

I approached the younger of the cops. "Hi, officer. I know this woman. Her name is Susan. Is there anything I can do to help?"

"No, not really. She's refused an ambulance, and has a girlfriend coming to take her to the emergency room. She's definitely been drinking, but I guess this incident has sobered her up a bit. We're gonna give her a break and just let her get to the E.R."

"Yeah, I guess a fall like this will do that."

The cop looked at me. "She didn't fall."

I was confused. "She didn't?"

"No. She was pushed by a guy wearing an orange sweatshirt. My partner and I saw the whole thing from our car parked across the street."

"Pushed? By who? Where's the guy? Did you catch him?"

"Not sure. We were here in less than a minute, but he was gone, just kind of disappeared."

"Shit . . . I mean, that's crazy."

"Sure is. There were a few other people out here, but they said they never saw him."

I thanked the officer for his help with Susan, and decided maybe it would be better if I didn't talk to her. She had a few people around her, and I was guessing Jackie would be the girlfriend that the cop had mentioned.

On my drive home I called Nick. He didn't sound good.

"I'm going crazy here, Michael," he said. "I'm trying to stay positive whenever I'm with Anna, but I'm scared, real scared. I just don't know what I'll do if anything happens to her. How can something like this happen to her? She's the best person I've ever met. And I'm angry. Very angry. I move around the house feeling like I want to punch out the walls."

I wasn't sure that Nick wanted to hear any platitudes at this point, so I decided my support would come in the form of listening. "I get it, Nick. I'm angry, too. This must be very hard on both of you."

He ranted for a few more minutes, then said, "I'm sorry, Michael. I didn't mean to dump all this on you."

"It's OK, buddy. I can only imagine what you two are going through. I don't mind at all. And it's better that you share your anger with me than with Anna, right?"

"I appreciate it, Michael. You're right. I don't want to upset Anna."

"Say, what if I come over tomorrow night and bring pizza. That way we can do some real catching up, and you can yell at me all you want when Anna's not listening."

Nick laughed. "Sounds like a good plan. See you tomorrow."

When I got home, my mom was sitting on the couch in her sweatpants and a long-sleeve T-shirt, her hair in a ponytail. When she put her book down, a bald woman stared back at me from the cover. "Good book?" I asked, sitting next to her as she put her arm around my shoulder.

"Yes, inspiring story about this woman and her battle with cancer. And she's got a wonderful sense of humor. How was the football? Was it tough watching it?"

"It wasn't as bad as I thought it was going to be. I met a nice guy there and we talked a bit as we watched the game. Somehow, I ended up spilling my guts out to him. It was weird. Sad thing happened with Jackie's friend Susan as I was leaving. She was drunk again and had a fall in the parking lot and is going to need some stitches. She got banged up pretty bad."

"Oh, no, that's horrible. I think about that young lady often. I knew her mom some years ago, and met her dad once or twice before he passed. The whole thing is just so sad." My mom sat, shaking her head, her lips pursed.

"Yep, sure is. I just wish she'd stop partying so much. I know Jackie is trying to support her, but nothing seems to be working. How can someone let themselves get so far down a hole and not try to get out?" I let out a deep breath.

"Michael, you're just really starting to get a dose of one of life's frustrations."

"What's that?" I said, sounding like a bored kid in a classroom.

She looked into my eyes, sitting up straight, "Honey, it's when we love someone and want to help and support them, and they're just not ready to receive it—for whatever reason. They're not ready to evolve, not ready to undergo some significant change." She bit her bottom lip before continuing, "That's one of the toughest frustrations to deal with."

I stared out the window, thinking about what my mom had offered and how it sure did sound like what Jackie was dealing with in Susan. "And how do you deal with it?"

Mom took a deep breath. "Well, I've just adopted the belief that we are all on our own journey. I've come to accept that I cannot control others and make them do what they're not ready to do. That's why I'm not riding you about your plans at the moment. I know you have to figure it out on your own so you can shape your own journey." She repeated it slowly as she took my hand, joining me in staring out the window. "Yes, we're all on our own journey."

CHAPTER 7

The Turndown

Success consists of going from failure to failure without loss of enthusiasm. - Winston Churchill

The next morning, I was up and out early. I hit the gym and did a full workout—weights, wind sprints, stretching—then went back home to change. Though I enjoyed working out, I didn't want to have only that to focus on over the winter. So some of my calls the previous week had been to friends in Pennsylvania, and I'd already had a first-round interview with a local asset management firm.

My fallback plan—or really, the fallback to the fallback, since I was still hoping to get into broadcasting if I couldn't play pro ball—was to enter the financial services industry. My college degree was in finance, and I had taken and passed my Series 7, or what's known as the General Securities Representative Exam, after my second year playing football. I had studied during my first two off-seasons, often in a Starbucks next to my apartment in Denver after my morning workout. I hadn't thought I'd need the degree or certification for at least another six years, but I didn't want to just mope around the house all winter.

The firm had invited me back for more in-depth interviews, so later that morning there I was, pulling into the parking lot of a California-looking building, its stone-wood-and-glass design making me feel like I was in Santa Barbara instead of a suburb of Philly. I turned off the ignition, took a deep breath, and reflected on my first interview. I felt like I'd done well, and the feedback from the interviewers seemed

I Met Jesus for a Miller Lite

positive—although the one woman had seemed more interested in the NFL locker rooms than me and my intention to gain a job with her firm. Maybe she could sense my heart was still back there.

Anyhow, I was replaying the first interviews and feeling good about my next interviews when I saw a black Range Rover pull into the parking lot. The driver pulled up to the spot closest to the front door, jumped out, grabbed an expensive-looking leather briefcase from the back seat and entered the building without looking in my direction. Thankfully, he didn't see me, because I didn't want to have to exchange pleasantries with someone I considered to be one of the most unpleasant people in town. *Damn! I didn't know he still worked here. I thought he'd moved on to a different firm. Wonder why I didn't see him when I was here before?* I considered not going in at all, but decided to take a shot since I was already there.

After a few minutes of focusing on the outcome I wanted from the two interviews I had that morning, I got out of my Jeep, put on my suit coat and headed to the front door past a few more European SUVs and sedans.

Erica, the receptionist, greeted me with a big smile as I entered the lobby. "Hi Michael, great to see you again, and glad you're back for more interviews." She got up from behind her desk and came past the copper-and-stone fountain with its peaceful sound. She gave me a hug.

"Hello, Erica, and thanks a lot. I'm happy to be back. You look amazing as usual."

"Thank you, Michael. Just trying to keep up with all you young people and stay conscious that age is just a number." She stopped, looked over her shoulder as she pushed a lock of silver hair behind her ear, and leaned in. "And if you ever let anyone know that I'm the grandmom of one of your friends. . . ." She paused. "Well, let's just say that this interview process will come to a screeching halt!" She laughed as she gently smacked my cheek. "Got it?"

"Absolutely, Erica. Got it."

I took a seat in the waiting room and a few minutes after 9 o'clock Erica came and took me to a conference room, where I spent two hours with three people from the firm who had not interviewed me the first time I was there. They asked the usual questions: where did I see myself in five years, what was my greatest strength, tell me about a challenge you've had and how you overcame it. It was a bunch of bullshit, and I think they knew it and knew that I knew it. They each handed me a business card on their way out and wished me the best.

I sat alone—silently—until Erica poked her head in the room and said, "OK, Michael, just one more. Let's go."

We walked down the hall toward an office at the end that was larger than all the rest and had a large silver nameplate on the wall next to the door. It was the name of the man driving the black Range Rover, a name I knew quite well.

Jon was on the phone as we approached his office door. He saw me, nodded to Erica, and motioned to me that it would be a minute and for me to come in and sit. Erica nodded for me to go in before she turned and walked away. I entered and closed the door behind me as Jon pointed to a chair and moved his hands to encourage me to sit.

I'd known Jon most of my life. He and I went to the same high school, although not at the same time since he was about six years older than I was. Like Jackie, he too came from a wealthy family. We'd known each other a little bit but he'd never paid much attention to me until I made it to the NFL. His office was full of framed diplomas, certificates and pictures of him posing with well-known business people or celebrities. His desk was clear except for an expensive-looking pen lying next to the neatly organized stapler, business card holder, and a paperweight bearing the seal of the Ivy League school had he attended. I smiled a bit, wondering, *Why does he need the paperweight when he has no papers?*

Jon had spun his chair around so his back was to me as I entered, but now he turned back to me, raising his voice a bit. "Listen, Pat, this is the final time we're having this discussion. Just do what I tell you and it will all be OK. The client will be happy, and they'll never know how we did it. Understand?" He paused a moment before moving his phone from his ear, holding it up in the air and hitting the red circle on the screen.

As Jon placed his phone on the corner of his desk, I noticed the picture next to it: Jon and three other men dressed in golfing attire, holding beers and smiling. Jon must have seen my look when I noticed Jackie's dad smack in the center with his arm around Jon's shoulders.

"Yep, great tournament yesterday, second-to-last of the season. It was the cancer benefit I saw you at a few years ago. I thought you might be there. I asked Jackie if you were coming; she rode with me for a few holes, since her dad wanted to walk a bit and get some exercise. You should have come."

"Yeah, I'm sure it was nice. I had some things to do with my mom, and then I just watched some football."

"Well, we were on fire. Finished 15 under and won first place in the scramble. We each got a free foursome for a round at Chantilly, as well as $400 to spend in the pro shop. I'll probably just give them to one of our junior people who can't afford to play there. All in all, a good day."

"Sounds like it. Didn't realize you played golf with Mr. Jennings, though I'm sure you know him."

Jon leaned back in his chair, running his hands through his short, stylish blond hair. "Oh, I've gotten to know Derek more the past few years. He's good friends with a partner in the firm, and I guess they were talking about my golf game, and it came up that I played in college and had a strong NCAA record. So he called last month and asked me to join his foursome in the tourney yesterday and a few more this fall." He paused. "Derek's a good guy. And you'll recall I met Jackie a few years ago when you brought her to the barbecue at my place. She's really nice, too. And a pretty good golfer. She hit a few just for fun yesterday."

I was certain he'd mentioned Jackie deliberately, knowing she and I dated . . . or at least used to date. My mind raced as I remembered that particular barbecue and Jon's obvious interest in Jackie even though he'd been engaged at the time. His fiancée had hung by his side, her low-cut top showing more than anyone really needed to see. I'd heard that the next Christmas he'd broken off the engagement, but let her keep the BMW he'd gotten her. *What was Jackie doing at the tournament yesterday? She never went to that one before. And why, now, all of a sudden is Jon friends with her dad?*

Jon pursed his lips, squinted a bit, and leaned forward. "OK, let's get down to business. Michael, I've talked with our teams about you and your interviews and want to talk about that, but before we do, what do you think about my firm? What do you think you could bring to us that will keep us growing and making money?" I breathed in easily and held an amusing thought about Jon referring to "my firm." I think I'd heard somewhere that he was just a minority partner.

I realized, too, that I had been right and shouldn't have come in when I'd seen him drive into the parking lot. I knew he was not going to offer me a job, and I was just fine with it. I'd do a whole lot of things before working for this ass . . . but I decided to have some fun. Fortunately, this was another game I knew how to play. "Jon, first of all, thanks for the opportunity to interview with Stonewall Asset Management." I felt good as I read his facial expression and his irritation that I did not say "your firm." *You arrogant son of a bitch.*

He pulled at the sleeves of his shirt and fiddled with his cuff links as I continued speaking. "Although I don't have a lot of experience in this business, I do have my Series 7, and I do believe I could generate some great relationships with some of my former teammates that could lead to bringing in some significant assets to be managed by us." I wasn't sure, but I thought I saw him wince a bit when I said "us."

"The one thing we share is our competitive nature—you with your golf, and me with football. Even though you played on the mini-tours for two years, and my career may be over after four years."

He shook his head. "Yes, and I was surprised to see you get up after that hit in Nashville. Guess I should be thankful golf is a non-contact sport." He grinned. "But yes, I'd agree with you that you certainly are competitive, and that's very much needed here at the firm for sure. But Michael, this is not football. It's not a game of brute strength. One has to have a certain intuition and focus on the business they grow, and the relationships that fuel that growth." He paused. "I guess I'd have to say this game of financial asset management is more like golf than football." He glanced to his phone as it began to buzz, let out a chuckle, then turned back to me.

What an ass. OK, Michael, keep your cool. Just wrap this up.

I nodded. "Yes, I can see what you mean, and where you're coming from." I rose from my chair, his wince confirming that I'd surprised him by standing. "Jon, I agree with you when you mention the importance of intuition—that sense of . . . of . . . of just knowing something. Intuition is extremely important in football, and I do believe I have a strong sense of it." He stood opposite me, his hands shoved in the pockets of his expensive slacks. "Here, I'll prove it to you. I know two things. Number one: You have no intention of hiring me. You've thought about it because then you could boast to people that you had an NFL player at the firm. You could also keep an eye on me and fool with me and at some point probably sabotage my career. And number two. . . ." I paused, enjoying the nervous curiosity written on his face. "Number two, you're an ass, Jon. You always have been and will likely always remain one . . . maybe even a bigger one as you keep making more money." I winked before allowing our stares to lock for a few seconds. I turned to walk out, no handshake needed. I had a number three as well that had to do with Jackie, but for whatever reason I stopped at two. All I can say is the look on his face was priceless.

On the way out, I stopped to give Erica one more hug and let her know she'd not see me for any more interviews. She nodded, smirking. "Probably a good thing for you, Michael. Why don't you go and take that handsome face and charming smile and do some TV work covering some sports and games? You'll do a great job." I smiled, remembering that DaVon had said much the same thing, then strolled to the front door as a young man in a navy suit with an expensive-looking leather briefcase over his shoulder entered. I took a guess that he was a recent college grad coming in for an interview. "Knock 'em dead, brother," I offered to him as he nodded, wearing a nervous smile.

The rest of the day? Well, let's just say it was interesting. Yeah, *interesting*, that word we use when we're not sure how to express ourselves. While I felt good in having been . . . what's that new word, authentic . . . with Jon—and guessing that I'd probably be getting a text about it from Jackie soon—it hit me again that I did not have a job. The problem wasn't so much the money. I was thankful for having had the opportunity to play pro ball after college and make great money, and I had been sure to save the bulk of it. Aside from taking Mom to Europe for a month a few years ago, I really hadn't splurged on anything. My Jeep was all I needed, and reasonable apartment living had been just fine for me, freeing up some cash to funnel into investments. The problem was direction and purpose.

I spent the rest of the day calling more of my old friends and former coaches connected with the NFL. Though my most realistic plan back to the American pro league took me through Canada, I decided to keep up my contacts with the NFL. *Because you just never know*. Mostly we relived some good times, but I know they realized I was trying to stay on their radar.

I even took DaVon and "Grandmom" Erica's advice and emailed my buddy Billy to get some momentum going with the TV possibilities. *Because you just never know*, I repeated to myself. Back in college, Billy and I had both minored in journalism and broadcasting. We'd managed to link every single assignment to sports. In the off-season, meaning any time I wasn't playing or practicing football, we'd even talked the campus radio station into letting us do play-by-play calls for any game going on—baseball, basketball, hockey, soccer, even track-and-field events. Later, we'd graduated to TV broadcasts, me in front of the camera and him behind it.

When I'd gone into the pros, Billy had gone into sports news full-time. He'd parlayed his passion and talent into winning a few Emmys, and had gotten me some guest-appearance type gigs on college games during my off weeks and the NFL playoff games (since my teams never made the post-season). He was very enthusiastic about having me throw my hat into the broadcasting ring.

The finest part of my day was absolutely the afternoon nap I took in the sun that poured through the window and onto Mom's favorite spot in the house. Mom was at work and let me know she was doing some volunteer work after, so she'd see me later when I got home from Nick and Anna's.

Around 4 o'clock I called Nick. "Hey buddy, we still on for tonight? I can grab a pizza or whatever you guys want, and come by when it's good for you and Anna." I was going to tell him about the interview but then just figured we'd cover it that evening.

"That sounds good, Michael, and pizza is great. How about 7 o'clock? Anna's napping now but should be up by then."

"Perfect. And tell Anna I look forward to seeing her."

A few hours later, as I drove up to their house, I saw Sheila pulling the front door closed behind her. She smiled and walked toward my car, giving me a hug as I got out.

Startled, I asked, "Hey, what's up? You OK?" As we pulled apart, I saw her tears.

She sniffed and wiped her eyes. "Sorry, Michael, I'm just so pissed." She shook her head. "And sad for Anna and for Nick. I guess it just hit me when I walked out, and then saw you." She paused. "You'll understand."

"I'm with you, Sheila, but understand what? How are they? You want to come back in? I've got a few pizzas here."

"No, no thanks. I've got a few things to do." She leaned in and kissed my cheek. "I'll be OK, just keep praying."

"OK, maybe some other time we can grab a bite, or a beer, or something."

Through her soft smile she said, "Yes, I'd like that."

I went into the house and joined Nick and Anna in the kitchen. We ate some pizza and Nick and I had a beer. Nick asked, "So how are you, buddy? How's the job search coming? You had an interview today, I think, right? How's your mom? And what's happening with Jackie?"

I could sense they didn't want to talk about themselves yet and was happy to fill in the gap. I took a swig of beer, shaking my head. "You really sure you want to know?" I laughed.

Nick leaned in with a serious look. "We do." I proceeded to tell them about my interview with Jon, and I'm pretty sure the slightest smile appeared on Anna's face when I told them about calling him an ass. I also shared the warm exchange I'd had with Mr. Jennings the other morning when I was leaving Jackie's place. I talked about my mom, my tryout in Canada and the potential for playing there next spring, and how my friend Billy might be able to get me into TV. I don't think I've babbled that much in my entire life. *This is what they need, right here, right now.*

When the pizza was almost gone, however, I decided to test the waters. "Anna, you look good. I mean, if I didn't know about the cancer, I wouldn't believe it." She wore yoga pants and a fleece top, and a white headband with a navy swoosh on it. "You look like you're ready to go run some 400s!"

She gave me a hug and told me about her upcoming treatments. "Ha, can't wait to get back to running again. But even so, I'm really good at the moment. I don't really have any pain or anything. And I have a feeling inside . . . kind of hard to describe . . . that it's all going to be OK."

"I'm glad to hear that, Anna," I replied. "I can see the serenity in your face and the longer you hold onto that, the better it will be."

Silence followed, then Anna gave Nick a special look. She seemed to be . . . glowing. She gave a slight nod and Nick turned to look at me. "Michael, we have something else to tell you."

"Wait, what else is there? Not more bad news?" I had the strange sense—that intuition I'd told Jon about—that this was the reason for Sheila's tears.

Anna came and sat next to me on the couch, taking my hand. "No, actually it's wonderful news." She looked to Nick, then back to me. "You know earlier I said I had a feeling inside that it's all going to be OK?" I nodded, tilting my head to the side. "Michael, that feeling is our baby. I'm pregnant." My eyes opened wide as I leaned back on the couch and put my hands behind my head.

After what seemed minutes but was probably seconds, I leaned on my knees and took her hand. "But wait, how did this happen?"

Nick stood and came to us. "Now, buddy, we don't have time to get into the specifics, but there is a book with illustrations of birds and bees. . . ." We were all standing now, and laughter took over. It felt good.

Through my laughter I said, "No, no, no. I got it, no need for details. You know what I mean. What did your doctor say?" We all hugged.

"Let's all sit down for a minute," Anna said. "Well, we found out because I've had so much blood work done, and some showed I was pregnant. Dr. Chelson told me we had options, but I stopped her right there and said, 'Doctor, we have one option. We're having this baby.'"

I looked at Nick; he nodded as his eyes filled. He tried to talk, but could not get the words out. Anna put her arm around him and continued. "Nick and I have talked with all our doctors and done some research, and it seems that there are many studies on pregnancy during chemo now because it seems women are waiting a bit longer to get pregnant . . . you know, with their careers and all. One study in Europe of 400 women found little to no evidence of a negative impact on the health of mom and baby when cancer and treatment was in the mix. Many of the babies weighed less at birth than babies from mothers who did not have chemo. But really no other side effects. Dr. Chelson just said she'll stop the chemo about three months before my delivery date."

"That's wild." I shook my head. "Just wild. Oh, now I understand what Sheila was talking about when I saw her on my way in. She was crying and said she was pissed about all this you are going through. She didn't tell me, but she said I'd understand."

We talked and laughed some more. When Anna began to yawn, I knew that was my signal. "OK, you two, I gotta get going." At the front door we hugged again. "You know. . ." I began, then stopped. "You know, this is gonna sound really weird given what you two are dealing with . . . but I just want you to know how happy I am for you. I love you both a whole freaking lot, and you're gonna be awesome parents." Tears came for us all.

I stepped out the door, then stopped halfway to my Jeep. I looked up at the clear sky, the darkness of the night speckled with bright stars, and was thankful for those two people in my life. And it felt good to be able to be there for them when their need was so great. My interview that day was nowhere in my thoughts.

Instead, I thought about my dad. After he left, my mom always had two priorities: her faith and me. She never really got angry about my dad, at least I never saw it; she'd just tell me as I got older that he was on his own journey. My dad and I had a relationship, but not the kind a father and son should have. He moved to Florida and got remarried. I'd met the new wife a few times, and she'd seemed nice. I guess my dad was happier with her. I often thought about what kind of dad I might be if something similar ever happens to me. I knew at least, that I would never be as good at it as Nick and Anna. They were both a lot more patient than I was.

I drove home. "Hi, Mom," I said as I walked in the front door and made my way to her for a hug.

"Oh, hi, honey. How was your day?"

I paused a moment. Mom looked at me and said, "Michael, that's not a good look you have working for you!"

I moved to the couch and sat. "Come on, Mom, let's talk for a minute." She sat next to me and I told her about my interview, and about the baby, and about how Anna had said it was all going to be OK.

"You think so?" she asked.

"I do, Mom, I really do. I don't know what it is, but I'm confident it will all work out." I kissed her. "Goodnight, Mom. I'm gonna head up to watch TV, then get some sleep. Luv ya."

"Love you too." She paused. "I just think . . . oh, nothing. Get some rest."

I watched TV for a few minutes and then said some prayers—reflecting on what Matt had said about praying to God, an external source of love, support and guidance; and connecting in union with the Spirit within me. The second was a different way of praying for me, for sure.

CHAPTER 8

The Past

Oh yes, the past can hurt.
But the way I see it, you can either run from
it or learn from it. – Rafiki

Over the next few days, I kept to my workout schedule and kept trying to work some leads to find a job. Early Saturday morning, I skipped the full workout, opting instead for a five-mile run as the sun crawled up over the eastern side of town. The morning rolled by. I spent most of it at Brew Ha Ha working on making more connections in the TV business. Billy and I did talk, and he let me know he was working on getting some interviews set up in New York for me in the near future. He also told me how to connect with some production people near my hometown so I could do some demo tapes.

I did a full workout in the late afternoon, then decided to reward myself with a burger at Harry's. As I pulled into the parking lot an hour later, my mind was racing once again. *This is weird. Why do I feel good? I have nothing solid on the job front. And it's unbelievable how many challenges Nick and Anna have in front of them. Yet I feel good.*

I remembered a guy who had spoken to my previous team about the importance of heart. He talked with us about the energy of the heart—the electromagnetic field, and that it can be measured up to 10 feet from the body. *Boy, Anna had some serious energy the other night, and I'll bet I feel good because I've got some residue from that.*

Inside, Jesse was moving fast and dropped a beer on the bar in front of me with just a wink. A guy in the corner played a really cool rendition of *Country Roads* on his guitar, altering the tempo between slow and fast. The pool tables were active, and the guy next to me was chowing down on a good-looking cheesesteak.

As Jesse made another pass, he dropped a bag on the bar in front of me. "It's from Jay. He dropped it off earlier this week for you. Said you'd like it."

As I opened the bag, I saw black. It was a New Orleans Saints hat, just like the one Jay'd been wearing. Only, when I examined it closely, I saw a famous signature in silver ink on the underside of the brim. I shook my head in amazement, removed the tag, adjusted the strap and put it on. The guy next to me, chewing some cheesesteak in the side of his mouth, looked over.

"Damn, that's a pretty nice gift to get. You a Saints fan?"

I smiled. "Thanks, yeah, nice hat. Good question. I didn't think I was, but I guess I am now."

"Well, looks good on your head, so I'd just say thanks when you see him." He returned to his cheesesteak.

Inside the bag was a bright white notecard, no envelope, just a card with the image of a sandy walkway to a beach in a deep purple ink in the top center of the card. Below, in the same color ink, was a message:

Hey, Michael –

Nice to finally meet you in person. I trust you like the hat—after all, we're all Saints in our own way.

See you soon.

I read the letter, taken aback by the kindness of this guy. Jesse stopped in front of me and asked, "What's up? Pretty nice hat Jay dropped off for you, huh?"

"All good. Just working on some job stuff, and got a good workout in, so thought I'd come see you and grab a burger."

"Sounds like a good idea," Jesse said, grabbing an empty bottle off the bar and flipping it behind his back into the recycle container without even looking.

"I was with Anna and Nick a few nights ago, just grabbed a pizza and stopped by for a few hours. She sure is one strong lady. They're both doing pretty well, and they asked me to say hi to you." I held back on telling him about the baby as I put both hands on the brim of my hat. "And yes, what a surprise from Jay."

"Yep, he's a good dude. He gave me a nice Saints T-shirt a few weeks ago, said he knows Brees pretty well and just needs to text him and he'll sign and send the gear."

"Do you believe him?"

Jesse nodded as a patron a few stools down signaled for his attention. As he began to walk away, he said, "Guess I do . . . he just seems like the kind of guy that always tells the truth."

"Yeah, you're probably right," I said to myself as I took a drink of my beer and got lost in thought about the life: getting cut for the final time . . . Canada . . . TV . . . but no job . . . Jackie . . . Anna and Nick . . . my new hat.

I was pulled back into the bar by a voice that came from behind me and close to my ear. "Nice hat, but too bad the Saints never called, maybe you could've been cut four times." I recognized the voice and turned, seeing Mr. Jennings taking a step back. Beside him was Jon.

"You know, I was even thinking maybe you'd get one more shot," Mr. Jennings continued, "until I figured you out and realized what you're all about. Heck, I heard even Canada doesn't want you! Just keep working on that resume."

I took a deep breath, glancing from Mr. Jennings to Jon, then back.

"You know, Mr. Jennings, I kind of thought I had you figured out too, but wasn't sure," I replied. "But now I do for sure."

"What's that supposed to mean?"

I shook my head slightly, and turned back to the bar, taking a sip of beer. I felt his stare on my back, and I'm pretty sure he wanted to provoke me so he could grab me or punch me. He'd never initiate it, and while he was in good shape for an older guy, I'd've had no problem taking him if needed. I was pretty sure no other guy in the bar could bench and squat what I could; and even if there were one, it was not either of these guys chirping in my ear. With all my anger and frustration, I could have kicked both their asses in a minute.

They made their way to the other side of the bar and sat down. Jesse walked over to me with a slight grin. "What was all that about? I thought I might have to come over the bar."

"Oh, nothing. Just Mr. Asshole doing what he does. Correction, two Mr. Assholes."

Jesse laughed. "Yeah, it's a shame. I always thought you and Jackie were a nice couple. You always seemed . . . what's the word I'm looking for?" He paused. "Easy. Yeah, you just seemed easy with one another. I see so much drama from couples."

As Jesse moved away, I noticed Jay had entered the bar and was headed my way, smiling and pointing to his head.

"Looks good on you," he said.

"Hey, Jay, thanks so much for the hat. I sure was surprised when Jesse gave it to me. How'd you get it?"

He didn't answer but instead gestured to the stool next to me, which had just opened up. "OK if I sit here?"

"Yep, sure. Just me, and let me buy you a beer."

"No need for that, but thanks."

"I insist. It's the least I can do since you got me this great hat."

"OK then, thanks. But I'll have it later if that's OK."

The bar began to get more crowded as Jay and I settled into a conversation about the Saints, the football season, and the weather. After about 20 minutes, he got his Miller Lite from Jesse, and toasted me before his first sip, "Thanks, Michael, cheers."

"Cheers." I clinked my bottle on his. "You really friends with Drew Brees like Jesse said?"

He took a swig, and turned to me. "Yes, we've known each other some time. Real good guy." He paused, watching me looking across the bar at Mr. Jennings and Jon. "So how's everything with you, Michael? It sounded like you had a lot going on the last time we spoke."

I was about to answer but saw Jackie enter the bar and head toward her dad and Jon. She looked fabulous in faded jeans and a white V-neck T-shirt. She kissed them both on the cheek and began to take the barstool next to Jon, when he got up and moved down one, letting her sit between the two of them. Jesse came up to her, blocking my view. As he moved to make her drink, Jackie looked my way and our eyes connected. She smiled sadly as she turned to her dad. I thought back to the photo in Jon's office. *Guess Mr. Jennings is fond of Jon's game. After all, Jon is a really good golfer, and Mr. Jennings is an ultra-competitive son of a bitch.*

"What's that?" asked Jay. I realized I must have spoken out loud. He continued, "Seems like there must be a good story here."

I turned to Jay and proceeded to tell him about Jackie and me, from when our relationship began during junior year of high school.

We'd both been good athletes, and in the beginning Mr. Jennings had liked me . . . or perhaps he liked telling people his daughter was dating an all-state running back. I took Jay through the college years and how we'd been a bit on-again, off-again, and how we'd dated other people.

After graduation we'd gotten back together and things had been good for a few years . . . so good that we'd even discussed getting married. But it was tough with me moving from team to team and city to city. That had been when my relationship with Jackie had begun to deteriorate and her dad had begun to see me as a loser because my career was not taking off.

"That's the word—loser—that he preferred to use," I told Jay. "Most times I heard it from Jackie as she recounted her dad's opinion of me, although he was kind enough to grace me with it personally a few times."

I'd known by then that Jackie wanted to stay close to her dad because she thought there was a lot of good in him. *Yeah, right. Goodness in Mr. Jennings is like the chance of ice in Hell . . . slim to none...and slim just left town.* I recounted the line to Jay, telling him I'd gotten it from my grandpop, who used to say it to me before games about the likelihood of the opposing team holding me under 100 yards rushing.

I looked across the bar. "And that guy, Jon, there with Jackie and her dad is a partner in a firm I interviewed with a few times. When I realized he worked there, I knew I wouldn't get an offer and I was right. And even if I had, I'd've turned it down." Shaking my head, I continued, "There's no way I'd work for someone like him.

"I think the rest you know from our chat the other day," I said to Jay. "Which means to top it all off, I am maybe not-so-gainfully unemployed at the moment. Hopeful about my prospects, but uncertain what my future holds."

I tipped my beer bottle at him, then changed the subject. "So how about you, Jay? What's your story?"

He smiled and turned to me. "Well, not nearly as exciting as yours," he said. "I grew up in a small town a few hours north of here called Bethlehem. I had a younger sister and older brother. Dad was a carpenter; my mom was a teacher, and she did a lot of volunteer work at our church and with the homeless people in the area." He paused. "She was a saint for sure."

"Did you go to college?"

"Yep, Lehigh University. Graduated with a major in Engineering and minor in Philosophy. I also took some Theology classes at a school called De Sales University over the mountain from Lehigh; had some really great Oblate teachers there."

I began to notice how peaceful Jay's face always was and how his eyes were always calm. The easy way he spoke intrigued me. "Oh, yeah, I know Lehigh and had a few friends that played ball there," I said. "Do you work now?"

"Yes, oh yes, I'm always very busy. I live just down the street in the big blue place on the corner of Aspen and Broad."

"Damn, I know that place. I love it. Great front porch."

"Yes, it's a wonderful place just to sit and be still. You'll have to stop over sometime. My work is not far away. I'm a software engineer at a company over in Blue Lake Corporate Center."

I looked across the bar, watching the trio eating nachos. Something inside me hurt when I saw Jon use his napkin to wipe something off Jackie's cheek as she smiled at him.

Jay followed my gaze, then turned to me. "Hey, listen, man. I know this just kind of stinks right now. But I want you to think about what exactly it is you're mourning. The relationship the way it really was, or the relationship you hoped to have." He put his hand on my shoulder, and I felt better. I looked briefly into his eyes. It's hard to describe, but I just felt peaceful. "It's all going to be OK, trust me," he said.

Jay slid a $5 bill to the end of the bar next to the empty bottle of Miller Lite he'd had. I offered to buy him another, but he declined. He stood, putting on a black flannel jacket.

Just then Jackie came up behind me and said hi. I introduced her to Jay and we made some small talk. As he said goodbye, I extended my hand to Jay, but instead of shaking it, he pulled me in and gave me a hug. Jackie just watched.

She sat down on the stool he'd left. "Well, that was weird. Who's that guy?"

"Oh, just a friend, real nice guy. Good to talk with." I paused and grinned. "Let's just say he gets it."

Jackie shook her head. "Gets what?"

"Nothing, nothing. Just a conversation we had."

"OK, whatever. So, how are you?"

Now it was my turn for a head shake as I glanced across the bar to see Mr. Asshole staring my way. "Come on, Jack, do you really care? Looks like you and Jon are getting along just fine."

She stood, looking at me with those eyes, and smelling the way she does . . . and I hurt so bad inside it was like someone was squeezing my heart. "Michael, just know this. I love you . . . always have, always will." She looked to her dad and Jon. "But this is probably the end of our romance. If I had to guess I'd say it's all about timing, and ours if off. Tell Anna and Nick I have them in my prayers." She smiled sadly and walked away.

I left shortly after that, the good feeling I'd had talking with Jay having faded quickly after Jackie's comments. Deep down I think Jay was right. I was feeling sad about the fantasy, the possibility of my relationship with Jackie. But that didn't make the loss hurt any less.

I chatted with my mom when I got home before turning in. I fell asleep that night visualizing a nice sunrise run the next morning.

CHAPTER 9

The Serendipity

Coincidence is God's way of remaining anonymous. - Albert Einstein

On Monday, my iPhone alarm went off. I barely noticed, since I was already wide awake. I guess you don't need an alarm when your heart's broken. Kind of hard to sleep with that. For a long time, I'd always thought that once I got more settled, Jackie would be there with me. But it wasn't to be.

I lay there another hour after the alarm went off, just thinking. Then I pushed myself up, got into my running gear, and headed out. The morning was perfect—clear and colder, although not cold enough for hat and gloves. The traffic was light as I took off down my mom's street. Most times I run listening to music, but that today I had enough to listen to in my head and figured I'd let it go where it wanted to go; it didn't take more than a hundred yards to be hijacked by thoughts of Jackie. My mind replayed some of the early-morning runs we'd taken at the beach over the years—sometimes on the road, sometimes on the boardwalk that ran along the shuttered storefronts, and sometimes on the hard sand, dodging the last bit of foam-topped water as it paused and headed back out to sea. I could see her now in my mind, with running shorts and tank top, headband and ponytail.

That little voice we all have in our heads started . . . *Man, what am I doing? I don't think it ever hurt this bad. What am I gonna do? I'm not sure I can be without her.* I slowed down as a black pickup truck drifted through the intersection. As I picked up my pace again, the voice echoed over and over. *I'm not sure I can be without her.*

My route took me past Harry's, and it sure looked different at 8:30 on a Monday morning. I'm guessing the lone beer bottle on the outside deck table had been left by a patron on their way out the door. There had been a few nights when Jesse and I had sat there after he'd locked up, talking about our lives. He'd been through a lot. Remembering his wonderful attitude about it made me smile and increase my pace.

Not long after, I came to a stop at the sight of a man coming out of a house just down the street. It was Jay, walking with a bounce in his step and a smile on his face. He glanced my way and for some reason I decided to duck down behind a bush. I peered out and was pretty sure he hadn't seen me. He got into a black Camaro, and soon its convertible roof rose up, then disappeared into the trunk. I smiled at the thought of him putting the top down on this chilly morning.

He was off down the road. And so was I . . . at a really quick pace. He turned onto Waverly at the light and I scampered across the street and through the backyard of the corner house. It was tough staying with him, but he hit a red light and I actually had to slow down a bit so he wouldn't see me in his rearview mirror. It occurred to me that he was probably heading into work as he made a left onto the road leading to a corporate park. My hunch was confirmed when the car's blinker went on and he turned into a parking lot, then pulled into a spot. I slowed to a walk, careful to be sure he didn't see me. He grabbed an old leather bag from the passenger seat, slung it over his shoulder and walked through the glass doors of a brick building with an 11 on it. He'd left the top down on the Camaro to receive the rising sunshine.

I sat on a low wall across the street, wiping the sweat from my face, and realized my ass was tired. *That's about the best workout I've had in a long time.* I laughed to myself. *I can't believe I followed Jay here. This is nuts. I'd better get home and do something productive like look for job, or else*

I may just become a professional stalker. I rose and began walking away, but then stopped. I don't know why, but I turned around and walked to the glass doors Jay had just gone through. I paused a moment and went in. A woman of about 60, with brown eyes and long gray hair in a ponytail, smiled at me as she spoke on the phone. She hung up and asked, "Good morning, may I help you?"

I smiled back. "Hi. Yes, thanks. I was just going to say hi to my friend Jay, who works here. I was out for a run and just saw him come in."

She pursed her lips and squinted. "Well, I'd like to help you, but no one has come through those doors in about 10 minutes. Until you just did, of course." She paused.

"Hmm. I could have sworn it was him."

She shook her head. "And not only has no one come in here, but we don't even have anyone named Jay who works here."

I shook my head. "Really? Are you sure?"

She seemed a bit irritated with me. "Yes, I'm sure. I've been here 10 years, and no Jays. Sorry."

"Oh, no, no. I'm sorry. I didn't mean to offend you. It's just weird." I'm guessing she thought I was a little nuts, maybe a lot nuts. "I'm sorry. Thanks for your help. Have a great day."

She smiled as I turned toward the door. "Thanks. You too."

I walked through the doors and immediately noticed the empty parking spot where the Camaro had been. I sat on a bench under some trees, lost in thought. *This is so weird. I know that was Jay! Am I going crazy? How could this have happened? And why would he leave again after just getting here?*

I was roused from my thoughts by the sound of a deep voice calling my name. "Hey, Michael." I looked to see a large dark-skinned man about my age walking toward me. "Michael? Michael Trumball?"

He was dressed in shorts, which seemed odd. As he got closer, he said, "Damn, it is you. I knew it when I came to the front desk and saw you walking away from the front doors. I asked Rebecca in there, but she said she didn't get your name."

I looked at the guy's face, trying not to look at the metal-and-black-plastic prosthesis that took the space where his right leg had been. "You don't remember me, do you?" He held out his left hand. "It's me, Ryan Barnett. I remember you because when I saw you walking away a minute ago, it reminded me of all the times you were running away from me and I was chasing you." He smiled at the hint he'd just dropped for me as I tilted my head looking for a memory. "We played against each other in two state championship games and that All-Star game our senior year." I took his left hand and shook it, noticing that he had a prosthetic right hand as well.

"Damn. Ryan Barnett, one of the baddest linebackers I ever played against," I said. "Man, you were a great player, and if I remember, an even better student. What's been happening with you?" He sat next to me.

"You're not cold? We can go inside," I offered.

He looked down at his shorts. "You're not dressed any warmer," he said. "I guess this isn't exactly a good outfit as winter comes, but a few of us from work here are volunteering today. We're gonna serve lunch at a homeless shelter, and it gets real hot in the kitchen."

"That's great. So what's up? What have you been up to?" I thought for a second. "You went to Navy, right? I sometimes thought I'd see you in the NFL."

A bright smile came to his lean face. "Damn good memory. Yep, went to Navy, then to Officer School, no pro ball for me. But I did follow your career. Well done on getting to the pros."

"Oh, thanks for the sentiment. I guess it was a good run, but after that hit I took a few months ago, that was about all she wrote for me and the NFL—at least for the time being. I'm hoping to play in Canada next season and maybe make it back to the NFL after that. I'd like to put in ten or twelve years in the pros. But I'm also exploring some other possibilities." I rubbed my hands together and cupped them, blowing my breath into them. "In the meantime, I decided to settle down here and spend some time at my mom's house."

He was shaking his head. "Yeah, I saw that hit, and I winced real hard at it. Man, I gotta tell you, I was cheering your name when you got up and walked off. That was badass. My wife came into the room when she heard me and watched the replay and I said to her, 'Yep, that's him. That's Michael Trumball. I knew he'd get up.'"

I laughed, "Thanks, but does it matter that I have no recollection whatsoever of walking off that field?"

"Hey, man, you walked off. In my book, that's what matters."

"So how about you? You work here?"

"Yes. I've been here about a year after I came back from my tour overseas, where I commanded some fine young Marines. Got a few mementos to remind me." He tapped his leg against the bench, making a clicking sound, and then gestured with his prosthetic hand. "I was given an honorable discharge."

I shook my head. "What happened?"

He took a deep breath, staring at nothing in particular.

"If you want to talk about it—if not, I understand." I said nervously.

"No, no, it's OK. I don't talk about it a lot, although people are always telling me I should share my story—that it will inspire others."

"I think that's a good idea. You sure you're not cold?"

He tilted his head sideways. "Marines don't get cold," he said with a straight face.

"Shit, right, my bad."

He smiled proudly. "Anyhow, I'll give you the short version, and maybe sometime we'll get together for dinner and we can catch up more. We were making a sweep through a town that had some really evil people there, the kind that you need to take out before they take us out." I nodded. "Now listen, Michael, I know there are a lot of people who want us out of there and want peace, and I do too. My wife is pregnant with our first child, due this spring, and I for sure don't want that baby growing up in a world with war and terror. But here's the thing—evil people don't want peace." I could hear how earnest he was in his voice and see it in his presence, his eyes and his face.

I was going to respond, but he spoke again. "We were moving through this town and were a few days in and almost finished when it happened. I was walking down a desolate street with four other Marines. The area had been bombed out, and a few cars sat deserted along the curb, outside some homes and shops. We were due to connect with other Marines in two more blocks, completing our sweep." He took a deep breath, looking up to the sky, then down at the ground.

He was talking to me but gazing out to the horizon. "Then it happened. A burst of automatic weapon fire came at all of us from below an old truck about 200 meters away. I saw two of my Marines fall and made my way as I returned fire. On my way to them, I was hit in the leg and fell to the ground. I got to my belly and returned fire as I saw one of our guys ready to fire a grenade. As I looked, I was hit again in my right forearm, pretty much just tearing it apart. It was all over so fast. The grenade landed and destroyed the truck, killing our attacker, and the moans of injured men filled the street. The sniper was alone; our other Marines were there in a minute to tend to the wounded."

He paused. "Lost some fine young men there, including Tommy. He played quarterback in high school in Tennessee and we used to love to talk football. He was only twenty years old and he died there in that shitty street." Ryan's eyes were moist.

Silence took over. A few people waved to Ryan as they walked to the front door. He waved back, wiping his eyes discreetly.

"Damn, I'm really sorry, Ryan," I said. He looked at me, as I sat shaking my head. "I don't even know what to say. I wish I'd heard about this."

He sat straight, his massive chest and shoulders rising as he took a breath. Then he exhaled and smiled softly. "You know what really sucks about this, Michael?" I shook my head, hardly breathing. "The sniper. He was only about fifteen. I often think about that day, and think if I'd only seen that kid in the street in a different situation, he and I might have been able to toss a football around. I would've loved to have had the chance to talk with that kid, and let him see me, not the big Marine with guns and grenades." He paused, then finished, "Just me."

I still had nothing to say, my mind racing to fill in all the blanks in his story, and his recovery and journey to where he was now—sitting on a bench with me in the small, safe town where we had both played football many years ago.

"OK, gotta get rolling," said Ryan as he stood. "It'd be great to have dinner, and maybe I can even bring my wife. You'll love her."

"Absolutely." Ryan took his phone from his pocket and asked me for my cell number. He sent me a text so we'd be connected.

I extended my left hand, he grabbed it and pulled me close for a hug. As we pulled away, he continued his grip on my hand, and looked squarely into my eyes. "Michael, it's been great seeing you, and I do trust we'll get together again. So until then, here's the thing." I nodded, uncertain of what was coming next. "When we first started talking, you said your career ended earlier than planned and you were having a problem deciding what you wanted to do even though you have some possibilities."

He squeezed my hand. "You sounded weak, my friend, and that's not the Michael Trumball I remember. Here's the thing about life. We all get hit . . . you by a linebacker, me by some bullets, others by sickness and disease, others by the loss of a loved one or child who died way too soon. But be assured, we all get hit, just in different ways."

He winked, letting go of my hand. "Are you a religious person?" he added. I nodded. "While we certainly always miss the people we've lost, what you have to remember then is that the hit really doesn't mean shit, it's just part of His plan. What matters is what we do with the hit." He looked upward briefly. "Life is about getting your ass out of bed every day, taking action, and being thankful for what you do have." His eyes were locked on mine. "And trusting that it's all gonna be OK. Got it?"

I stood taller. "Yes, Ryan, thanks. I think I got it." I watched as he walked back to the doors, his right leg making a unique sound on the stone walkway, his right hand swinging easily.

I turned and began the final leg of my run home at a fast pace. When I got there, I grabbed a quick shower, checked some emails and decided to take my laptop to Brew Ha Ha and do some research on stats for both NFL and CFL players. I wanted to keep in touch just in case I got a call.

CHAPTER 10

The Second Chance

Watch what you wish for;
you just might get it. - Anonymous

Against all odds, I ended up going to Canada. The player rep for the Saskatchewan Roughriders called and told me about an injury to their running back and uncertainty about the veteran second-stringer. He offered me a game-to-game contract, and mentioned the potential bonus for advancing to the playoffs and Grey Cup. I said yes almost before he had finished speaking.

The day I was leaving, I rose, grabbed breakfast with my mom, and then said goodbye. I loaded my bags into my Jeep and pulled out of the driveway. I turned off the radio, thankful for the external silence as a hurricane of confusion raged internally. For some reason I was thinking about that conversation with Jackie and her talking about timing. *Is our timing off because of me? Because her dad is an ass? I mean, as long as he's in the picture, I cannot see the timing—as she puts it—ever getting better. Yeah, I gotta follow up with her on that timing comment before I leave again.* Maybe that's why my car automatically headed toward her townhouse.

I coasted down a road that led to a small parking lot on the left filled with cars. I was looking for a space when I suddenly hit the brakes, coming to a stop with my passenger side tires in the grass. Backed into the spot in the corner was a black Range Rover. I knew it was Jon's; any doubt was removed when I saw the license plate facing my direction: UNDERPAR. *Shit, what's he doing here?* The energy drained from my body, and I had a strong feeling of loss.

I'm not sure why it hit me so hard. I'd been struggling with the impending truth that it was over with Jackie. I released the brake, rolling forward down the road that looped around the back of Jackie's building. It was probably the strangest feeling I've ever had when she peered over her coffee mug, sitting in a chair on her deck, feet in Jon's lap. The morning air was cool but comfortable, and the flames from her gas fire pit danced in front of them. She wore plaid flannel pajama pants and the old gray hoodie that I'd given her years ago with the Billabong logo on the front. Our eyes locked and her expression never changed as I drifted around the bend.

Just before we lost visual contact, I saw her left hand rise slightly off the arm of her chair and give me a peace sign. That was our word, PEACE. We'd often talked about that's what we really desired . . . peace in our lives, and she liked to wear the silver necklace I'd given her with that word engraved on it; she always said it was her favorite. Jon never looked up from his phone. Thoughts raced as I felt trapped in a slow-motion movie scene. *Shit. Shit. Shit. What was I thinking? This is the dumbest-ass thing I have ever done. She's got to think I'm the biggest loser. Shit.*

Though I'd only planned that one stop at Jackie's on my way to the airport that morning, I found myself making another. Minutes later, I was kneeling in a pew toward the front of St. John's. I knelt for probably half an hour, going back and forth between prayer and thoughts about Jay, Nick and Anna, my career, my mom and, yes, Jackie and Jon. I got up and dropped a bill in the metal box and lit five candles on the rack at the foot of the statue of Mary, and knelt there for a bit, just talking with Her and asking for some support.

Then I returned to my pew and sat, eyes closed, breathing very slowly.

I felt a hand on my shoulder, then heard a feminine voice say, "Hey, Michael."

I turned. "Hi." I paused, surprised and not sure what to say next. "What brings you here?"

"Probably the same thing that brings you here. Well, maybe not exactly." Susan slid in next to me, giving me a brief hug. "I've come to realize that I can't keep going down the road I've been on. I'm on my way now to check into a house for women battling addiction. I guess I just stopped in here to ask for some help ... some ... support I guess, in this next chapter of my life." She smiled softly.

Very suddenly, I felt a release of all the animosity I'd held toward Susan. Instead, I reached out and took one of her hands. "I'm glad to hear that, Susan." She didn't pull away. "I think this was a perfect place to stop. And I want you to know that we all seem broken at some time in our life. Maybe confused, or broken, but we just know the world doesn't have the answer . . . so we come here." I nodded to the sanctuary around us. "Would you like to talk about it? You don't have to if you don't want to. We could just sit here quietly."

"Michael, I'm broken, for sure, and I need help. Ever since my dad died, I've been on a downward spiral, and I just don't want to feel this way anymore. It kind of reminded me of when Nick and I went out for a while in high school, and then he broke up with me just before he went to college. It's a shitty feeling. I know I was jealous of Anna when she started coming around, and I did some bad things to try to get him back." She let out a slow breath. "I guess I was just a bitch."

She smiled sadly as she stared toward the front of the church. "I'll always have a special place in my heart for Nick, but believe me when I tell you I really do want Anna to get better and for her and Nick to have a great life."

Susan turned to me as her tears began to flow. "I'm sorry for the crap I've done to you and a lot of other people. I just miss my dad so much." She wiped away a tear. "So much." She pulled a napkin from her jacket. "What I've been doing lately to deal with the pain—getting wasted and sleeping with different guys to feel like I'm loved again—is no way to live."

I put my arms around her. "It's OK, Susan. I want you to trust that it will be OK." After a moment, she took a deep breath, wiped her eyes, and sat back in the pew.

She looked straight into my eyes. "I'm not sure why, but I think I believe you, Michael. I'm going to trust that it will get better. Well, it could hardly get worse." She gave a small laugh, then looked up to the large crucifix hanging behind the simple wooden altar. "I will get better."

I wiped a tear from my eyes. "You will, Susan, you sure will." I got up to leave. "And let me know if there's anything I can do."

"Thanks, Michael, I will." We hugged and I walked a few steps toward the back of the church, leaving Susan in the pew, her head bowed. An odd feeling came over me and I stopped, turned, and walked back to her, placing my mouth close to her ear. "And Susan, your dad's Spirit is with you also. You have to believe that." She didn't move. "Your dad will be with you every step of the way." She turned, unable to talk, her eyes filled, her bottom lip quivering, a smile spreading across her face. I turned and walked down the aisle and out the large wooden doors.

Several hours later, as the plane took off for the first leg my journey, Philly to Toronto, I reflected on my morning, and the excitement about my next few weeks waned. I tried to stay busy on the second flight to the city that would be home for the unforeseeable future reading the playbook I'd been sent and becoming more familiar with the differences between the CFL and NFL. *The longer and wider field may just be good for me. And I never wore green and white as my uniform colors, so maybe this will be good and bring me some luck. I wonder how Anna and Nick are doing today.*

After landing in Regina, I was quickly into a cab and off to my apartment, thankful that the lease was month to month. There was just another month to go in the regular season for the CFL, and it was likely I'd get some playing time in all the remaining games. I knew from my research that the team was playing well and had their eye on advancing to the Grey Cup championship in late November.

My sleep was restless that first night in the sparsely furnished apartment. I was quick to get moving in the morning, getting a cup of coffee at the Tim Hortons coffee shop on the corner opposite my apartment building, then grabbing an Uber to the practice facility. The next few days went well as the coaches complimented my quick learning of the plays, as well as my speed and strength. I stayed in touch with my people in the U.S., and was happy my mom was stopping by to bring food to Anna and Nick twice a week. Nick texted me how much that meant to him, and let me know that Anna was doing just OK, but would be returning to the hospital in a few weeks for more treatment.

My first game in Canada was a victory, as the Roughriders scored a season-high 42 points. I played about half the game, getting 11 carries for 68 yards and nearly breaking a long run in the fourth quarter on which I would have scored and gone over the 100-yard rushing mark.

I called Nick nearly every day and got updates on Anna. Her chemo had started (and she was going bald, as she'd predicted), but so far she and the baby were both doing as well as could be expected. Still, I had to fight an urge to jump on a plane and go back to be with them.

The next game was another win and my playing time and statistics improved. Optimism about the playoffs was high. The coaches were playing me more since the first-stringer was still out and the backup, Dante, continued to struggle through his third knee injury. Dante was older than me and had played in the NFL for six years before finding a home in Saskatchewan.

Texts from my agent became more frequent, all suggesting how he was working to get me a few tryouts back in the States next season, and for me to keep up the strong play. I didn't respond to most of them. Despite my success, my heart seemed to be back in Pennsylvania.

The day before my third game with the team, I was sitting in the Tim Hortons coffee place, feeling alone and longing for a morning at Brew Ha Ha. I'd talked with my mom the night before and she'd picked up on my sadness. "Michael," she'd said, "you don't sound very good for someone who's going after his dream and is actually playing very well." I told her I was OK, just feeling a little tired.

We won again, and a week later we were about to play the final regular-season game. Because of the Roughriders' recent winning streak, this game was important as the playoff scenario unfolded. If we won, we'd have a chance for the playoffs. But our fate depended on the outcome of the Calgary Stampeders game. If they lost and we won, we'd get in, but if they won, our game didn't matter.

I was dressing at my locker when my attention was called to Dante at the locker two down from mine. He reached into his bag and removed a syringe. With the skill of a surgeon, he inserted the needle into a bottle, pulling back and filling the syringe with the clear liquid. He noticed my stare, and with a slight smile and a wink, he proceeded to inject the fluid into this knee in three places. He put the needle and bottle back into his bag and stood, bending his knee a few times. "Just gotta make it a few more games, then I can get it fixed again."

I went back to getting dressed. While that was not the first time I'd seen a player stick a needle into a part of their body, now something was different. I suddenly felt weak. My head ached, and thoughts of home and the people there stormed into my mind.

The game went great. Dante was having a strong game, and the team was driving down the field, trailing by one score. With just over a minute left, I was sent in to give Dante a breather. The quarterback called the same pass play that had ended my time in Nashville. The play unfolded the same, with me catching the ball and turning to run, although this time I was not hit. I was in open field with the nearest defender angling toward me from about 15 yards away. The goal line was in sight and I started running toward it, the crowd roaring with the anticipation of a tie game. I made a move to switch the ball from my left hand to my right. The ball slipped toward the ground, and bounced off my right foot to career directly toward the approaching defender. He bent down like a shortstop and easily scooped up the ball and blew past me on the way to his goal line. Fumble. Touchdown. Game over.

After our game, most of the players headed to a restaurant to watch the Calgary game. I got a lackluster invitation to join them, but turned it down and instead went home to beer and pizza. I didn't watch the game, but checked my phone when I knew it should be over. The Stampeders won the game convincingly, making our loss irrelevant and securing their spot in the playoffs by knocking the Roughriders out. So the fact that I'd fumbled and lost our game—in theory—really didn't matter. But in reality, it did. I knew that my focus just wasn't on the game of football anymore. At least not right now.

A few hours later I grabbed my phone as I sat in my apartment, a beer bottle sitting in a small puddle on the table in front of me. The text I sent to my mom's Realtor friend, Mary, was short.

> Hi Mary, this is Michael Trumball. If that house you showed me a few months ago is still on the market, will you put an offer in for me. Asking price is fine, no need to negotiate. And please don't say anything to my mom, just between you and me for now. Thanks.

I finished my beer and a few slices of what the Saskatchewan folks call pizza. On my way back from the fridge with a fresh beer, my phone buzzed on the table.

MARY: Hello Michael, great to hear from you. I can make the offer now, and we should be good, but the older couple selling this home is ready to come down in price. Should I wait?

ME: No. Tell them I'll pay full price, cash.

MARY: OMG. I'll call them right now. You will make their day, probably make their year.

ME: Good. I haven't done that in a long time. Text me when you hear. I'll be home Tuesday. Thanks, Mary.

CHAPTER 11

The Return

God will either protect you from suffering or
give you the unfailing strength to bear it.
– St. Francis de Sales

The following Tuesday morning, I was on the first flight out of Regina International, certain I was leaving Canada behind for sure this time. Mom and I had talked after the game, and as usual she was her loving, supportive self, telling me not to worry about the fumble and that I had played well enough up there to get another look at the NFL. I responded, "Thanks, Mom. We'll see."

I smiled at the thought that she had no idea what I was planning. Mary had called me and we had indeed made the older couple's day. Our plan was for me to get over to Mary's office and sign the papers after I landed back in Philly. All the inspections were done and the sale was agreed to by all parties.

A few minutes after five o'clock, I jumped out of my Jeep and hustled into Mary's office. I was happy, but felt like the pen I was using to sign so many papers would run out of ink any minute. Finally, we were finished and after the teary hugs from the older couple, I was standing with my coat on, holding a packet of papers.

"Well, Michael, you have yourself a real nice house there. And I'm sure you'll do a wonderful job with the renovations. I'm glad it worked out," said Mary as she gave me a hug.

"Yes, Mary, I think you're right. And thanks for helping me with the setup with my mom tonight."

Mary grinned. "Yep, probably one of the best little white lies I've ever told. As soon as you leave, I'll text her I'm on my way to O'Leary's and will meet her there. You better get going so you can get there first."

A few minutes later I was sitting at the bar in O'Leary's, facing the front door. I saw her before she saw me, which was perfect. She scanned the booths for Mary, and her eyes went past me, then came back quickly as she put her hand to her mouth and hurried my way, saying loudly enough to cause some stares, "What in the world are you doing here?" We hugged tightly, finally pulling apart. "What's going on, why are you here? You said you were coming home next week. I'm here to meet Mary for dinner."

I smiled as the bartender placed a champagne glass in front of each of us and popped the cork on a bottle. "Mom, just sit, just sit down. I'll explain it all. Mary's not coming. I've been with her for the past hour." I slid the folder her way.

She looked down at the folder then back at me, shaking her head. "What? What?"

"Mom, just open the folder."

Her hands shook as she opened the brown folder. She pulled her glasses from her pocket and began to read. After a few seconds she exploded, "Oh my God. Michael, this is the greatest surprise ever!" She reached over and gave me the tightest hug I've ever received. We toasted with the champagne and had a wonderful dinner.

The next few days were busy. I got a few texts from Nick that Anna was hanging in there. I was running around doing a lot of things related to my job search and new house. Saturday morning, I was having breakfast with Mom and just talking about life. Our chat was interrupted by a call from a woman named Tara, who was the VP of a sports channel.

She knew Billy and wanted me to come to New York the following Monday to meet with her and discuss some possibilities.

Having a TV gig would be great, I thought. I'd still make good money but be able to spend more time at home with everyone. I emailed Tara back saying I'd take the train to New York on Sunday night, stay in a hotel, and meet her Monday morning—knowing it would be a full day, because she'd said we'd spend time in the studio doing work in front of the camera.

That afternoon, I grabbed a quick cup of coffee and some fruit, then changed and took a run before heading off to see Anna. As I knew from the phone calls while I'd been in Canada, she'd been doing OK with the chemo, but now she'd checked into the hospital so the doctor could keep a closer eye on her and the baby as this round of treatments was coming to an end. Nick told me she was being allowed visitors that afternoon and that he'd be there with her. I wanted to make sure to drop in at least once or twice before heading to New York.

Nick was in the chair when I entered Anna's private hospital room. He looked as tired as he'd sounded over the phone. The strain was showing on him as well. He was sad, lacking the simple, joyful energy he'd radiated for so many years.

Only two flower arrangements sat on the windowsill; a lone balloon hung in the corner of the ceiling. Nick looked up.

"Hey, buddy, how are you?" I whispered, not wanting to interrupt Anna's rest. She was thin, and her face had a grey color to it. Dark circles colored the skin beneath her eyes, and she was indeed bald. I wasn't sure how she could sleep with the hissing, dinging and beeping of the machines standing like sentries around her bed. Nick just shook his head, then leaned forward and ran his hands through his hair.

He looked up, then stood, getting very close to me as he led me into the hallway. He leaned against the wall next to the water fountain as an older woman slowly passed, wheeling a machine attached to a pole next to her. Nick looked from her to me.

"Michael, I'm exhausted, and I can only imagine what Anna feels. She just fell asleep, but she was complaining of the worst headache she ever had. This is so goddamn unfair." He paused, shaking his head, hands stuffed into his pockets. "I've tried, but man it's getting tough to stay positive. I just want this to be over and for us to be home, happy, and having a baby come spring."

His tears came as he continued. "I just want to drink a bottle of wine with her and fall asleep in her arms after we make love. That's what I miss the most, just holding one another. Then I want us to wake in the morning"—he wiped his eyes and sniffed loudly, causing the older woman to stop and turn back to us—"and make her an omelet."

I put my hands on his shoulders as he continued. "Is that . . . is that really too much to ask? I've been praying my ass off since this nightmare began, and the Big Guy upstairs just ain't making anything happen. Can't you see how she's gotten worse since you went to Canada?" He was silent, taking deep breaths to calm down. Then he whispered, "I feel like I'm at the end of my rope."

I began to talk. "Come on, Nick, it's gonna. . . ." I stopped. My heart told me Nick did not want to hear it was "gonna be OK." He didn't want to hear "hang in there, be strong." He just wanted to be heard. So I gave him a hug then stepped back, then we went back into the room.

Nick wiped his tears, patted my chest and fell into a chair in the corner. Before leaving, I bent to kiss Anna's forehead, and whispered the words I hadn't said to Nick. "Hang in there, Anna. It's going to be OK. Be strong."

I left the room silently, thinking I hadn't been there enough for Nick.

As I walked down the hall and started to pass the nurses' station, I stopped. The older nurse sitting behind the desk looked up from her iPhone. Her hair was short and gray, and her eyebrows were thick, like my grandfather's before he passed. "Yes? Can I help you?" Her tone was cold, and the energy in her eyes was unwelcoming. She sort of reminded me of an old nun I had in seventh grade. I could never understand how that nun could be so miserable every day. A friend of mine used to laugh and say that the nun would probably have been happier if she'd been a prison warden instead of a nun. Grade school humor, right?

I was put off by her tone but decided to lead with love. "Yes, thanks. I'm sorry to interrupt you, and sure do appreciate all you do here for these patients, and especially my friend Anna down the hall."

I thought, but couldn't swear, that I actually saw Audrey—that was the name on her tag—relax her shoulders and smile just a little. "It's OK, not interrupting me at all."

"Thanks, I just wanted to ask you quickly about Anna. Is there anything you can tell me, or anything I can do to help?"

Audrey stood and glanced at a few monitors down on the desk after they made some beeps, then down the hall toward Anna's room, and then back to me.

"I can't tell you anything about her condition because that's private," she said. "But I can tell you she's a tough one. I've been here 34 years, and she is probably one of the top three toughest patients I've taken care of. Doesn't complain about anything. Always has a smile for the staff. We are all trusting for the best."

"Well, thanks, Audrey. Just keep her in your prayers, OK? Have a nice day."

Audrey smiled slightly, turning back to the computer screen. "You too."

I walked down the hall, gazing out the window at the beautiful winter day and the few bright-colored pots full of winter greens that sat along a hedgerow, contrasting sharply with the azure sky. I was reaching for the elevator buttons when a shrill voice pierced the air.

"Help, somebody, help. Get a doctor." The voice was violent, desperate. It was Nick. He came out of Anna's room, eyes wide, screaming for help, his white shirt spattered with red. I got to the room right after Audrey. Anna was unconscious on the floor with blood running from her nose and a gash on her cheek. Her body was shaking, and Nick's eyes were unlike anything I'd seen before.

CHAPTER 12

The Questions

Press on. – St. Paul

In an instant Anna's room was packed with nurses and doctors. The looks on their faces betrayed their fear, frustration, and life-or-death urgency. I was ushered out of the room, and took my place leaning against the wall across the hall. The door to Anna's room was closed, but I could see Nick each time someone entered or left. The door opened, and two nurses, one guy I didn't know and Audrey were trying to get Nick through the doorway. He was screaming he wanted to stay and howling Anna's name over and over. I wrapped my arms around him as he turned and looked at me with desperate eyes, sobbing as we both fell to our knees.

"Come on, buddy," I said, rocking him to the rhythm of his sobs, as his tears and snot covered my shirt. "Come on, buddy, hang in there for Anna. She's gonna be OK."

A doctor came out of Anna's room and bumped my shoulder with his knee, never turning to see what he'd hit. There were so many people running around, and so much medical jargon . . . prep OR . . . call for plasma . . . *stat* . . . and orders being barked. Nick looked up at me, wiping his nose on his sleeve. He let out a loud scream, then looked at me. "She just woke up and tried to get out of bed. She fell right onto her face before I could get to her. If she dies, I don't know what I'm gonna do, I'm telling you, Michael. . . ."

I grabbed his face firmly with both hands. "Stop, stop." He took a deep breath. "Look, Nick, you need to calm yourself down. Anna needs you." Another deep breath. "Come on, let's get out of the way and let these people take care of her." I pulled him up and we made our way to a bench down the hall.

Soon a doctor came over to talk with Nick and me. He said they had to take Anna to the OR to "see what was happening." Nick just sobbed and buried his face in my shoulder. A minute later we joined a bizarre parade of people wearing blue scrubs and white coats, all following the stretcher as it rolled down the hallway carrying our precious Anna. A skinny man banged the wall plate to open the stainless doors. Audrey stepped into the middle of the hall and stopped Nick and me. "You can't go in there," she said. "Just go back to the waiting room."

I took Nick's phone and looked up the numbers for his parents and Anna's parents. I made the calls and told them they should come to the hospital. Nick sat next to me, leaned his head back against the wall and just stared. I looked at his arm poking from his rolled-up sleeve and noticed how skinny it was. I thought, *This has been pretty tough on you, buddy. I'm sorry. I'm here for you now.* I quietly stood, then headed to the nurses' station down the hall and asked Audrey for a scrub top so Nick could get rid of his stained shirt before the parents arrived. Nick let me change his shirt, obeying orders to lift his arms but not helping otherwise.

Both sets of parents arrived with other family and friends, and the wait began. As the hours dragged on, the crowd dwindled, with people conveying their wishes and prayers, then taking their leave.

Finally, late into the night, Dr. Chelson came from the OR toward us with a man in navy scrubs, a mask hanging around his neck. Both their caps were soaked with perspiration. I roused Nick and gave him a little smile, handing him a water bottle as he rubbed his eyes, his stained T-shirt invisible to all as it sat in the trash can in the corner. Dr.

Chelson hugged Nick, then separated and asked him and the parents
to come into the small private room off the waiting room. They led the
way, and Nick turned to me, then said softly to Dr. Chelson, "I want
Michael to come too." She nodded and entered the room, followed by
the other man and the rest of us.

She began, her eyes focusing first on Nick as he sat motionless in a
chair, then working their way slowly to the rest of us. "Nick. Everyone.
Anna had a brain aneurysm." Both moms gasped in unison and quickly
moved to their husbands' outstretched arms. Nick took a deep breath,
and then put his face in his hands. Dr. Chelson walked to Nick, placing
a hand on his shoulder. After a minute she knelt down, her face just
inches from his. She took his hands, gently pulling them away from his
face.

"Nick." His head stayed down. She placed two fingers under his
chin, slowly pulling up until their eyes locked. "Nick, we need to talk."
He nodded as the parents and others moved close like players returning
to a huddle.

"Anna is stable. She did well in surgery. But she's in bad shape. She
had what's called a subarachnoid hemorrhage; it's what happens when
an aneurysm ruptures."

Anna's mom sobbed quietly. Nick's mom moved in and took one
of Nick's hands. Dr. Chelson continued. "Dr. Ali here is a fine surgeon,
one of the best." She turned to the man, who nodded humbly. "He was
able to stop the bleeding and repair the damaged blood vessel, but what
she needs now is rest." She paused. "Rest and time."

Nick wiped his eyes and sat back. His bottom lip quivered as he
spoke. "And the baby?"

She looked at me, then to Nick. "Her treatments were putting
strain on the baby." Dr. Chelson paused. "And now this." She stopped,
the silence allowing my thoughts to turn to the worst. "For now, the

baby's OK. The best thing will be the same . . . rest and time. We'll have Anna in an induced coma for some time. She'll be unconscious so will not be able to communicate with you, so just know this when you're in there. And trust me, it's best for now."

"How long?" Nick stood, his mom coming closer to hug him as his dad placed his hand on his shoulder.

Dr. Chelson said it would be at least a week, maybe more, and that it was best for Anna and the baby.

Nick looked to Dr. Ali. "Thanks, Doctor, for what you did for Anna. She's been so strong throughout this, but now. . . ." Nick began to sob. "But now, I just don't know . . . I just don't know."

Dr. Ali took a step closer. "Nick, she is strong. Let's just let Anna rest, and give it time."

Nick's dad added firmly, "And prayers."

Dr. Ali smiled softly. "Yes, that is good too; there is much healing in our prayers. The best thing for Anna and the baby is for the brain to heal, and that takes time." He told us the room Anna would be moved to and let us know it was OK to move to the waiting room and hallway nearby.

I stayed with Nick a few more hours, until carts stacked with breakfast trays rolled by in the hall. People moved around the room, leaving to come back with water bottles, coffee and food. The table in the corner looked like the college breakfast buffet I remembered from finals week. No one really talked much, and the bloodshot eyes of the folks were a constant reminder of the pain and sadness.

"Hey, buddy," I said. "I'm going to head out. I promised my mom I'd go with her to Mass today, and then I have to prep for my New York trip tonight. I'll try to stop in this afternoon before I catch my train. I may have to stay in New York a few days. Billy got me in to see the VP of a sports network, and it sounds like I have a real shot at a TV gig. You going to be OK?"

Nick took a deep breath, rolling his head from side to side. "I'll be fine, Michael. I'm happy to hear you have this opportunity. For now, my mom and dad really want me to go home and get some sleep, so that's what I'm gonna do. They said I'll have to be ready when Anna wakes up. They're going to rotate shifts with Anna's folks so that someone is with her at all times."

We stood. His stare was unnerving. "Nick, you're gonna be OK, right? I'll bag this trip if you need me," I said.

"No, you go . . . you go." He looked down the hall, and said some words I didn't quite believe. "Yeah, you go. I'll be OK."

CHAPTER 13

The Realization

Call it intuition, call it sixth sense. Call it anything you want, but just know that sometimes we just know.

Though bleary-eyed, I went to Mass with my mom—thankful I'd had the chance to play again in Canada, thankful for what that chance had taught me about my direction in life, thankful I'd gotten the interview. But mostly, I thanked God for the fact that Anna was hanging in there.

After Mass, I grabbed a quick nap then decided to go to Brew Ha Ha before heading to the hospital to visit Anna and Nick. I pulled my Jeep into a spot and walked into the coffee shop. A young man with white cables dangling from his ears nearly ran me over with the overflowing trash can he was sliding across the floor.

"Tony!" screamed a young lady from behind the counter. He looked up. She nodded toward me. "Keep an eye out and lower your music. You nearly ran this guy over." Tony pulled out one of his earbuds. "Hey, sorry, man," he said to me.

"All good, you're working hard. Have a good day." He smiled and turned the corner, still dragging the trashcan.

"Hi. Sorry about that. Can I get you something?" the girl behind the counter asked. A pen stuck out of her blond ponytail, and she wore an easy smile.

"Oh, that's OK. Don't worry about it. Yes, can I get a medium coffee and an everything bagel, toasted, with a little cream cheese? Please."

"Sure." She turned and walked away. I spun around when I heard someone call my name, and shook my head when I saw Jay in a leather chair over near the front window, legs crossed, sipping from a mug. He was motioning for me to come over. I gave him an I'll-be-there-in-a-minute sign. *Oh, this ought to be interesting.* I took my change and dropped some bills into the larger glass jar on the counter, stopped at the old wooden table to add some cream to my coffee and walked to the chair next to Jay.

"What's going on, Michael?"

I settled into the chair next to him, and got comfortable. I smiled as I turned to him. "You know Jay, I was going to ask you the same question."

Jay took another sip, and looked back at me, a soft smile on his face. "Well, I guess this is it. I figured we'd get around to this conversation."

"You did? And what conversation is that?" I took a sip of coffee and began to scrape some cream cheese from the abundance on my bagel.

Jay placed his mug on the table and leaned in. "Michael, you want to know why the woman at the office the other day didn't see me enter, nor did she know me."

I shivered, nervously placing my mug on the table. I was going to speak, and it seemed Jay knew this, but I could not get words out.

"Michael, it's OK. It's all good."

We were silent for a moment. Jay watched two women walk in, the younger supporting the arm of an older one who was using a cane.

I shook my head, thinking back to my interactions with Jay, and more about his with others. "Don't take this the wrong way—" I began.

I seemed more relaxed now, although I wasn't sure where the calm came from. I shifted in my chair. "Ever since I met you, I've noticed a few . . . how shall I say it . . . weird things."

"Like what?" Jay said as he ran his fingers back through his long hair.

"Well, I guess first was that Sunday when we first talked at Harry's. Those guys were getting ready to fight. Then you walked by and touched the one guy, you know, the one with the muscles who was really pissed off." Jay nodded. "And then you left and it seemed like something came over that dude. Not a minute after that, he walked over to the guy he was gonna punch in the face and shook hands."

"That was good. Nobody needs to be fighting and angry over a game of pool. I guess it was just a coincidence that he realized that a moment after I walked by."

I looked at him quizzically. "Yeah, maybe. But what about that little baby's arm in the coffee shop?"

"Yep, we discussed that. Seems he just took a tumble. What about it?"

"Here's 'what about it'! That little kid's arm was broken. You know it and I know it. It looked like a damn hockey stick for crying out loud." I realized my voice was sharp and loud when a guy a few tables away glanced over his shoulder. I leaned in and dropped to a whisper. "And then you grabbed it and held it for a few seconds and it was healed. And finally, I see you walk into a building with my own eyes, then no one else has any notion of that, and then your Camaro is gone, it's just . . . just gone. Poof, into thin air." I gestured with my right hand to match my point.

"Continue."

Again, there was a strange calm about me. "And then, well, ever since I came back home, I've had a feeling that something drew me here. That I was supposed to be here at this time. And not just to help Nick and Anna. So let's start with some easy questions. Number one, how do you know I followed you to the office building and that I went inside and talked with the woman at the front desk? And number two, why did she not see you? Third, why was your Camaro not there when I came out?"

He finished his coffee and looked intently into my eyes. "Yeah, nice car, huh?" he winked. "It was not there because I moved it a block away to sit in it and watch you talk with Ryan."

I felt the blood drain from my face. My calm was replaced by a queasy stomach and dry mouth, not even wanting to talk about that. I was going to say something about Ryan when another memory crashed into my consciousness, causing me to shake my head, take a deep breath and rest my head in my hands.

I think Jay noticed. "And what's that all about?"

I continued slowly. "I don't know, I'm not sure, but I just have a feeling you may know something about it." He nodded for me to continue. "After that night we first met in Harry's, as I was leaving, I came across this woman—"

"Susan," he interrupted.

"Yes, Susan. She was on the ground. I thought she was drunk and had fallen until I spoke with a cop and he told me he and his partner were across the street and that she didn't fall, but was pushed down"—I paused—"by a guy in an orange sweatshirt."

Jay looked away, then back to me. "Yes, Susan was knocked down. I was there and saw it."

"Well, shit. I knew it. If you were there, why didn't you do something? You should have helped her."

"We did."

"We. Who the hell is 'we'?" I said sharply.

He leaned in, and spoke slowly. "Michael, Susan was knocked down by her dad."

I sat back, stunned by his last comment, my head throbbing. "Susan's dad is dead. He died in a car accident on his way to see her graduate from Clemson," I said. And then the goosebumps came. "Whose school color is . . . orange," I finished softly. Jay nodded slightly, then walked to the counter, returning a minute later with a steaming mug.

"You OK?"

Another deep breath and I said, "Not really. I don't know what to think." After a few seconds I continued, "Jay, her dad is dead. How? I mean why would he knock her down? And how could he?"

His face was devoid of emotion. "Michael, it's like this. We both know Susan is struggling in life, and understandably so. Her abuse of alcohol to cope with her dad's death is not the best choice, but again, I get it. Many people go that route to ease the pain, or numb out. But that does not create healing. When she was about to get into her car, there was a young woman a few blocks away driving a sedan with her baby girl in the back seat. Susan's dad knocked her down so she didn't drive drunk and hit that car"—he paused before finishing—"and cause more loss."

I had no feeling in my face, or arms, or legs, just numb, sitting in stunned silence. "But how?"

Jay answered my question quietly and simply. "There's a fine line between here and there."

We both turned to the window, and I know I was staring at nothing, trying to process what I knew was true—from the way I felt when Jay said it. *There's a fine line between here and there. But how? This is crazy. What the, what am I supposed to do now?*

I finally turned back to Jay. We looked at each other, until I spoke. "Jay, what do I do now? Why did you tell me? Am I the only one who knows?"

"Yes."

I stared into my near-empty mug for another minute, then looked up slowly. "What about Ryan? You led me to him."

"And what do you remember of that conversation?"

"He talked about how everyone gets hit by something in this life. And that we all have to learn to cope with our own hits, rise every morning, and be thankful that we can."

"What did you think about that?"

"I think he's right," I replied. "I hadn't thought about life . . . about my life especially . . . that way before. And now I've been thinking about his comments ever since and trying to be more balanced in how I frame my own situation."

"Good to hear. So you went for a run and ended up learning a life lesson from someone who's been hit a lot harder than you. Not a bad deal, right?"

I nodded slowly, the rest of my body remaining very still.

A thought had formed in my mind. A thought that sounded both crazy and obvious at the same time. "Are you . . ." I took a deep breath. His eyes never left mine, and I could feel the peace within them. "Are you . . . ?" I could not finish my question.

He smiled and stood. "Yes. I am who you believe I am." He held out his hand, "Nice to meet you, Michael."

We hugged, an unknown but welcome peacefulness invading my entire body as he said into my ear, "Michael, have faith . . . trust. It's all going to be OK. It always is."

I shook my head. "Wow." I paused. "And what am I supposed to do now?"

"How about this? You go on about your day. Let all this settle, tell others, don't tell others. It's your choice. We'll see each other again soon."

"OK, OK, sounds good. I still can't believe it."

Jay turned to the door, then looked back. "Yes, I'm a little disappointed you didn't get it sooner." He paused and winked. "I mean, I even told you I was from a small town called Bethlehem and my dad was a carpenter. But relax, you're not the first to miss me when I was right next to you. And I'd like it if you continued to call me Jay." He shook his head, laughing softly as he strolled out the door.

I nodded, laughing myself, then fell back into my chair as my eyes followed Jay out the door. I headed off to the hospital, stayed with Nick for a while, then went back home to shower and rest up before heading out.

CHAPTER 14

The Choice

Pray that you will not fall into temptation.
- Luke 22:40

That night my mind raced as I stared out the window as the train sped north toward New York, the sun long since hidden below the western horizon. *I wonder if Anna is going to get better and if Nick can hang in there. He's always had such a strong faith—much stronger than mine. This is the first time I've seen it waver. Wonder what Jackie's up to? I'll bet she's gonna go skiing out west with Jon over the holidays. Damn. What's this interview gonna be like? And Tara? She sounded cool via the emails. Guess we'll just have to see.*

I walked to my hotel from Penn Station. Though it was just early November, the storefronts were filled with lighted Christmas trees, presents, and Santas. The streets were filled with people doing what people in New York do . . . work, shop, sightsee.

Nick had told me that Sheila was going to take a turn staying with Anna that evening, so I gave her a call. She let me know Anna was stable and resting well, and the doctors were pleased. She was still in bad shape, but hadn't regressed at all, which was something everyone was keeping an eye on. I told her what a good friend she was to Anna.

She replied, "Well, thanks for checking in, and have a good trip. I'll text you if anything changes, but I'm thinking she's OK for now." She paused. "I know things look bad right now, but I have a really good feeling that she's gonna be OK. I went to meditation class today after I left the hospital, and me and the guy I told you about offered our meditation to Anna and sent her healing energy. When all this calms down I still want you to come to a meditation and meet Jay. I think you'd like him. Gotta run, luv ya. Bye."

I can only imagine what my facial expression was when she said "Jay." I stopped, causing a man to walk into me from behind and utter some curse words. I yelled into the phone, "Wait, Sheila, Sheila, don't hang up yet. Wait. Sheila." But she'd hung up. I thought about calling her back, or maybe texting her but decided I didn't want to get into that after the past couple of weeks I'd had.

I gotta get this TV job. I need something good right now. I need this.

The next morning, I walked to the restaurant to meet Tara for our breakfast meeting. I don't remember much about that walk, since I was still brooding about Sheila's mention of Jay the night before. As I approached, the door opened and two men in overcoats and scarves hustled past me with no acknowledgement. I heard one of them say, "This will be good, nice to make a few million for the holidays." The other just winked.

Inside, a waiter in a white jacket approached. "Good morning. Mr. Trumball, I presume? Miss Smith is waiting for you." He motioned for a younger woman to take my coat. "Please, this way."

We set off through the crowded tables that were covered with burgundy cloths that blended with the dark carpet and mahogany walls. As we approached a corner booth that was large enough for six people, the woman there looked up from her phone and smiled at us. She slid from the booth, turning first to the waiter. "Thank you, Manny." She extended her hand to me. "Good morning, Michael, it's nice to meet in person." She was tall and tan, and her shoulder-length blond hair contrasted with her black V-neck sweater.

"Hi, Tara," I said as I felt her strong grip. "Thanks for meeting with me. I appreciate it."

She sat down, motioning for me to slide in across from her. "I'm sure you can imagine how many ex-players contact us to do some TV work." She shook her head. "Just seems like we've set the expectation that they can make millions like the Fox guys." She looked directly at me, a slight smirk on her face.

"Would you like coffee?" she continued.

"Sure, thanks."

She nodded to Manny. "I hope you don't mind, but I took the liberty of ordering for us. Just some fruit, yogurt, granola and pomegranate juice. We've got quite a busy day and we have to keep moving."

"Sure, sounds good. Tara, I just want to . . ."

She held up her hand, "Michael, I know, got it. Just tell me why you're here and why you think you'll be good for our ratings."

I stumbled through my reasoning. Tara kept cutting me off to share her insight and observations. As hungry as I was, it was difficult to eat. She skimmed the bottom of her bowl, getting the last bit of yogurt, then put the spoon in her mouth and pulled it out slowly before pointing it at me. "Michael. Here's the thing. You have got to appeal to both the men and the women watching. And I'm going to invest in you for the day to see if you can do that. I'm going to get you some time in front of the camera, and if you do well, we'll continue to the next step."

Manny came with the check and she handed him her credit card.

She kept her gaze on me the whole time. "You know why I thought you might have potential?"

"I think I do, but I have the feeling you're going to tell me."

She smiled, squinting a bit. "Good, good. Yes. You're a handsome guy and fill out that suit well—although we may have to work on your coloring a bit. You're not exactly a household name, but you played in the league, know a lot of the players, and I'm told you've really studied the game and can make watching interesting for the fans. Plus, what intrigued me about you is that you survived that hit. That's going to make a great clip when we introduce you." Her lips pursed as she glanced from me to the credit card receipt on the table. She signed with a few quick strokes and stood. "Let's go."

I followed quickly behind her, my mind racing in a million directions as usual. *I can't believe she saw that hit. Man, she sure is all business; I'll have to stay focused today. I wonder how Anna and Nick are doing? Hopefully Tara will give me a break at some point today so I can check in with them.*

Once out the front door, we jumped into a waiting car and moved through the crowded city streets, weaving in and out of lanes as the heat from the leather seat moved into my butt and legs. Tara was on her phone, apparently checking her voicemails. She put down the phone, then turned to me.

"So you've done the prep work I emailed you about?"

"Yes, I appreciate that."

"Good." She turned back to her phone, her thumb making quick strokes up and down. I stared out the window, wishing I were in sweats headed to practice instead of in a tight-fitting suit in the middle of this city.

My day with Tara and her team resembled the shopping malls at the holidays—lots of hustling, loud voices, emotions, and stress. Before I knew it, I was behind a desk in the studio, with a taped football game playing and a guy named Pete next to me. Tara sat in a chair behind the center camera, interrupting and barking instructions for the next few hours

At the end of the morning, she took me aside and said, "So what do you think?"

"Good day so far. Your team is great. They made it easy for me to look good in front of the camera."

"I think you're right." She picked up a remote control and hit a button. Suddenly there I was large as life on a big-screen TV. She played a few minutes of one of my test runs.

"Not bad," she said. "Not bad at all, especially for an amateur. With a little polishing, I think you have a real shot."

"Thanks, Tara. I've worked hard on this, and I'm glad to see it's paying off."

"So . . . are you interested?" She continued before I could respond. "Of course you are, right? I mean, what an easy job—do some prep, show up, look good, talk football, and get paid a lot of money."

"Yes, I'm interested."

"I figured." She glanced at her silver watch. "You've done well enough that we're going to put you through the next phase where you get to meet more of the people you'll be working with. I have a meeting for most of the afternoon. In a few minutes my assistant will bring you some lunch, and then take you around. Then we'll meet back at my office later this afternoon. Right now, just relax and do anything you need to . . . text, email, calls. Whatever." She was out the door before I could say anything, leaving me staring out over the rooftops lit by the midday sun.

I texted Sheila to see if we could talk. She got back to me saying she'd call in a few minutes.

I went to check my emails just as another text vibrated my phone.

Hi Michael, this is Jay, I got your number from Sheila and wanted to let you know I've got Anna and Nick and all of you in my prayers. Peace.

I stood and moved to the window, shaking my head. *Now I'm getting texts from . . . from Jesus. I've got to put this number in my phone. But wait, what do I put it under? Jay? Jesus?* I stretched my neck from side to side and let out a small laugh. What else could I do? *Shit. This is really crazy. Instead of praying for Anna, why doesn't he just visit her in the hospital, just make her better, and then the baby can be born healthy, and we can all be done with this nightmare?*

Tara's assistant brought me a tray with some sandwiches and fruit. I'd just taken a bite when my phone vibrated. "Hey, Sheila, thanks for calling. What's happening there?"

"Hi, Michael. No problem, I got here about 20 minutes ago and was actually allowed to go into see Anna for a minute. She's doing OK in terms of not having any setbacks, but she's pretty much like she was yesterday. Nick was in the room, actually yelling at a nurse. Can you believe it? I've never seen him like this."

"OK, got it. Guess it's good she's not had any complications."

"Yep," Sheila replied. "The doctors and nurses keep saying that she just needs time. And that as she heals—her brain heals—that's what the baby needs." She paused. "I'm just scared for the both of them . . . and Nick too. He doesn't look good and his nerves are running really ragged."

My stomach tightened. I breathed in deeply. "Yeah, I know, I noticed the same thing yesterday. He's always been so positive in the past." I paused. "But I guess we all have our breaking point. I'm probably more worried about him than Anna, since she has 24/7 care and attention, and I'm not sure Nick has any."

"Yeah, I . . ." she paused. "Hold on. Here comes Nick. You wanna talk with him?"

"Sure, good idea, put him on." I heard Sheila tell Nick it was me, and then heard a sad and strained voice that I hardly recognized.

"Hey, Michael."

"Hey, Nick. Sheila just filled me in on Anna. Seems like she had a good 24 hours."

"That's what they're telling me," he said with a tinge of despair. "But she's not getting better. I just want her to open her eyes. I want her to hold me."

I took a deep breath and told myself to be positive with him and not rip into him about getting his act together.

"Nick, I'm sure you're exhausted, and I'll bet—in some way—that Anna knows you're there. Just hold onto that as you sit with her."

"OK."

"I'm not sure when I'll get out of here. Tomorrow at the latest. I'll for sure come to the hospital when I'm back. But if you need anything, you just call, buddy. OK?"

"I guess. Text me when you're on your way, although I'm sick and tired of all the phone calls and texts I'm getting about Anna." He stopped, then added, "I even got one from Susan. It got me thinking about the old times and how much fun she and I had. And then I felt even worse for going in that direction with my wife lying in a coma just a few feet away. . . ."

"Steady on, Nick. I'm sure you're tired from a lot of this. Just maybe get a nap now. I'm sure you've had a long day. You have to get some sleep."

"Yeah, OK. I'm not sure what I'm going to do. See ya."

I heard the phone getting passed back, then Sheila's voice. "Hold on, I'm gonna walk down the hall." There was a pause. "OK, OK. See what I mean? Probably a good idea for you to get home as soon as you can."

"I will. Thanks, Sheila. For sure I'll be back tomorrow, but maybe I can swing a train later tonight, just not sure. See you later." As we hung up, I pondered bringing up the text I'd gotten from Jay, but from a place of fear, confusion, or whatever . . . I didn't. I wonder what Susan's text to Nick said.

Tara's assistant returned, and I began a series of meetings, or I guess they were really interviews. After the fifth one, where two of Tara's people told me how the contracting and compensation was done, I was taken to a small conference room and told I'd be seeing Tara in about 15 minutes. I looked at my watch. Six o'clock already. *Long day. But I think it went well.*

I took the opportunity to call Nick. No answer, and the message said the mailbox was full. I tried Sheila. No answer there either. I stared out the window at the city lights, my heart racing a bit and my stomach queasy.

I was led to Tara's office. As I entered, I tried to calm my mind, attempting to deal with what was happening at home as well as get some focus for what was happening here.

She stood gazing out the window of her 40th-floor office, airpods looking like misplaced earrings hanging from her ears. She was talking fast and loud, motioning for me to sit at the glass table.

"Please, please, just get this done," she said to whoever was on the other end of the line. She walked to her desk and touched the phone with her finger, then took a seat across from me, crossing her legs.

She looked up from some papers, removing her stylish reading glasses. "Michael, you did good today. Some things to work on, but an OK job. All my staff think you have potential, and that's not something they say about many people."

"Thank you."

"Here's the deal. I'd like you to stay in the city tonight. I know you had a hotel room last night, but I've switched you to a different place, one much closer to here. After you check in, you will go to a tailor shop a few blocks away to get custom fitted for a suit, shirt and tie I have waiting for you. You're on your own for dinner. Be back here at seven tomorrow morning for a breakfast meeting with me and two colleagues who will be in on the decision about whether to bring you on formally and start grooming you. You might want to know that we've also been in talks with that quarterback from Colorado who won the Heisman about seven years ago but didn't make it in the league either. He was in a few times to audition." She paused. "He's good, and, frankly, my colleagues like him a lot. But maybe, just maybe, I can influence their decision if you're here."

She held out a card. "Here's the hotel where you're staying. I wrote the name and address of the tailor. He's expecting you and will make any alterations if needed while you wait."

I stood, taking her extended hand, fighting back my temptation to decline by explaining to her about Nick and Anna. "Thanks, Tara. I really appreciate it. See you in the morning." She smiled, nodded and turned back to her phone.

I got my coat and headed for the elevator. As I stepped out into the cold night, I wrapped my scarf around my neck and set off toward the hotel named on the card. I pulled my phone from my pocket and noticed a text from one of the last people I expected: Jesse.

> Hey Michael, just wanted to let you know Nick's here. The place is nuts and game time is still 2 hrs away. He seems really down. He said you were in New York. Just wanted you to know. I'll keep an eye on him.

I ducked into the lobby of the hotel, dialed Nick's phone and heard that message again that his message box was full. "Shit," I said in a whisper. Instead of heading to the front desk, I sat on a leather bench just inside the front door, and rubbed my forehead. The doorman, an older guy who to me looked of Hawaiian descent and who wore an easy smile, asked, "Hey, my man, you OK? Need some help?"

I looked at him. His lips closed, and his eyes locked on mine.

"Yeah, yeah, I'm OK." Then for some reason I continued, "No, no, it's not OK. I think my best friend's not doing too good." I paused, "I guess you can help if you want. You can pray."

I was shocked at my words, having no idea why I was telling a complete stranger about this. I stood as he made his way to me and wrapped his arms around me, the smell of a nice cologne filling my nose. He pulled away, our eyes still locked on one another. "Oh yeah, I can do that, I'm really good at prayer." He finished slowly, "He's going to be fine."

"Thanks." I looked at his nametag. "Thanks, Abraham."

"Of course, I'm here if you need anything." I texted Jesse as I made my way back to the street and turned for the tailor's shop just a block away.

> ME: OK, Jesse. I've got to stay the night here now, but will be back tomorrow. Keep an eye on him.

> JESSE:

I was greeted by name by the tailor as I entered his shop. His black hair was slicked straight back and he wore expensive-looking shoes, pants, and vest. My guess about his heritage was confirmed when I saw the familiar boot-shaped form of Italy in his silver cuff links.

"Michael, glad to meet ya. I'm Anthony. I did some research on you after Tara called, you know, lookin' at your Wikipedia and getting your dimensions. I figured you couldn't have put on much weight since that hit was only a few months ago. You look good." He held out a beautiful navy suit, motioning to the dressing room. "This should fit like a glove. Go ahead and try it on."

A few minutes later, I came out of the dressing room and fell under the precise eye of Anthony. He said nothing, just circled me like a shark and its prey. "Hmmm," he said as I felt the chalk in his hand make a mark on my butt and across the center of my back. "Good, go ahead and take it off and give me 20 minutes. You can have a seat over there, and there's some Sambuca behind the counter if you want a taste."

I smiled. "Thanks, but I'm OK right now."

About 20 minutes later Anthony returned, handing me a garment carrier that contained the suit, the freshly pressed shirt, and the tie. "You should be good to go." I went for my wallet and Anthony stopped me. "Nope, it's all good. Tara's got it."

"You sure?" I asked as Anthony tilted his head.

"Yes, I'm sure. Enjoy. Think of it as a very early Christmas present, Michael."

"Thanks, Anthony." I handed him a $100 bill. "Merry Christmas to you too." He winked before helping me on with my coat. Out the door, I'd begun to retrace my steps toward the hotel when my phone lit up. I froze. It was a text from Jesse.

> JESSE: Nick's still here. With some of his old high school guys. Susan is here too. She and Nick look pretty close.

My thoughts were flying. *Susan, shit, shit. What's she doing there? She's supposed to be in that recovery program. Damn, what's happening?* I texted back.

> ME: Is she drinking?

> JESSE: Looks like it. She's holding a beer and a shot now. I'm trying to keep an eye on them, but we are slammed.

I looked at my watch. About quarter after seven.

> ME: OK, thanks. Don't let him leave. I'm heading that way
> now and can maybe make it before halftime.

That was the last I heard from Jesse. I tried Sheila, but got no answer. I left a message, then recalled she was working and probably wasn't checking her phone.

I looked up and saw the smiling face of Abraham. I hurried to him. "Abraham, I need a car back to the Philly area. Right now. I don't care about the cost. I never checked in, but I understand someone brought my bag over from the other hotel. Perhaps it's being held at the desk?"

He nodded, and walked into the hotel, barking an order to a bellboy. He was back immediately, and gestured down the street toward a limo parked near the corner. "Got a car right here, Mr. Trumball." He gestured with an open hand, and the driver pulled up then got out of the car. He was a man about my size and probably in his forties.

"Sean, my friend, this is Mr. Trumball, and he needs a ride back to the Philly area."

Sean shook my hand. "Nice to meet you, sir." He hung my garment bag in the car, then took the bag that a bellboy brought out.

Abraham spoke to Sean. "You need to drive fast."

"Is there any other way?" He winked at me.

I turned to Abraham, slipping a $100 bill into his hand "Thanks."

He grinned, nodding to Sean who was standing next to the open back door. "My pleasure, Michael. Glad our paths crossed. Godspeed."

Once in the car I called Tara, getting her voicemail, and explained as best I could that I was on my way home to help a friend and would have to miss tomorrow morning's meeting. A few minutes later I got a text from her.

I hope he's a pretty good friend. You know how many guys would've loved to have had the day you just had? Sorry, but the decision will be made tomorrow and it won't be you. Keep the suit, you'll look good in it and can wear it to your next interview. 😊

I shook my head at her reply. *Damn, she sure is a tough one.* I thought about calling Jackie, my thumb poised over her name on my phone screen, but then just dropped the phone on the seat next to me and put my head back, closing my eyes.

On the drive back to the Philly area, Sean and I talked about his kids, his football days at a small college in Connecticut, and some about my career—I found it interesting he didn't mention the hit. He talked about how he did a lot a volunteer work at the youth center in his hometown. "It feels really good to be helping out these kids. They're great kids and just need a little guidance and attention. I like being able to contribute that way."

"I get it," I replied. "I've been thinking more and more about that very idea lately." I went on to tell him about Nick and Anna, about my stint in Canada, and my search for a new direction in life. Finally, I said, "In the back of my mind, a little voice is starting to take over. Ever since Anna's diagnosis, football has begun to seem less important to me. I still love the game, and I'm bummed about missing out on doing the television commentary, but I think I'm gaining more perspective now. I spent the last four years getting paid very well to carry a ball down a field. It just doesn't feel as fulfilling to me as it did before. Shouldn't I be doing something to be of service to my friends and family? My community?"

Sean replied that he saw a lot of benefit from giving people a form of entertainment and release through professional sports. We ended up in a lively debate, and before I knew it, the 90 minutes had flown past and we were entering the outskirts of Philly.

There'd been no texts from Jesse or Sheila, so I was a little nervous as we pulled into the lot at Harry's. Sean said he'd wait for me. I jumped out of the car before it had fully stopped. The bouncer smiled as I rushed through the door, pushing through the crowd and making my way to the open service area of the bar as it presented the fastest access to Jesse. He saw me coming and placed a bunch of beers on the bar in front of a crowd wearing football jerseys.

"Hey, man, I'm so sorry. Nick and Susan left about an hour ago. I grabbed my phone to call you and, just as I did, the busboy knocked into me as he was moving a trash can, and my phone ended up in the full sink."

" Where'd they go?"

"I don't know, but I'd have to guess both Nick and Susan had a good buzz going. They seemed very . . . um, close."

I spun around and went out through the side door to the deck, jumping the railing to get quickly to Sean's car.

"What's up?" he asked, dropping the limo into drive.

"We have to get to Nick's." I gave him directions.

Sean moved the car across town like an Indy 500 racer, running a few red lights after looking both ways. We turned onto Nick's road, my shirt moist with sweat, not from the temperature, but from nervous energy.

"OK, Sean, right here behind . . ." I paused. "Damn, behind Susan's car."

I opened the door as we came to a stop. I reached into the front seat and dropped a wad of money into Sean's hand before getting out. "I can't thank you enough, Sean. I'm good from here."

"Sure. I'll stay if you want, it's not a problem," he said as he pulled my suitcase from the trunk, handing it to me as I walked toward Nick's front door.

"No, thanks. I'm set." I was a few steps from the car when Sean rolled down the passenger window and hollered, "Hey Michael, what about this?" He held up the garment bag.

I turned, bending down to see. "Keep it. You'll look good in that suit."

He smiled and held up his thumb as the limo sped away.

Moving quickly up the front walk, I noticed the glow of the kitchen light spilling into the front room. My mind was racing. *Shit, what should I do? I hope the door is unlocked. I should never have gone to New York.*

Nick's baseball cap lay on the ground on the front stoop. I opened the screen door and noticed the key still in the lock of the main door. I peered in the front window, but saw nothing. My hand reached for the key, and I jumped back as the door opened and Susan stood there, one side of her face eerily lit from the glow coming from the kitchen.

I exploded through the door. "You bitch. How could you do this? You know Nick's not in a good place." I glared at her, bumping her shoulder as I moved quickly into the house. I stopped in my tracks when I saw Nick sleeping on the couch, covered in a navy blanket, snoring softly, his shoes on the floor. I went to him, tears filling my eyes. "Sorry, buddy, sorry." I knelt next to him. Susan moved to the chair across the room and sat quietly.

A few minutes later I turned to her, seeing that she was clear-eyed and not the least drunk. I tried my best to convey my apology through my eyes. She motioned to the front door, and I followed her out to the front stoop, picking up Nick's cap and taking a seat next to her on the black iron bench.

I took her hand. "Susan, I'm so sorry, I just thought. . . ."

She interrupted, putting two fingers over my mouth. "Michael, Michael. It's OK. I don't know what you've heard about tonight, but

I can understand what you were thinking a few minutes ago. Nothing happened."

I shook my head. "But why are you here? How are you here? I thought you were in the program. And Jesse sent me a text that you were drinking. He saw you with a beer and a shot."

Her dark eyes looked back to me. "Yes, I guess to Jesse it would have looked like I was drinking, but I've not had a drink since I saw you in church that day." She took a deep breath, pressing her lips together as she exhaled. "For some reason—and I know it sounds weird, and it was for me, trust me—for some reason I had the feeling I needed to leave the program tonight and take a drive. I thought I was just driving aimlessly, but I ended up at Harry's. I wasn't going there to drink . . . at least I don't think I was. I know it sounds weird, but it was like something was pulling me there."

She put her other hand in mine. "Anyhow, when I got there and saw Nick, and the fact that he was partying, something came over me . . . something really good. He was drunk and flirting with me, so when some of his buddies were into an exciting part of the game, I made my move and got him out of there. The beer and shot Jesse told you I was holding was Nick's."

"Oh, Susan, I'm sorry, I'm so damn sorry for what I said . . . and what I thought. Thank you for taking care of him."

"Yeah, sure. It was good to take care of someone . . . I'm so used to it being the other way around." She laughed a little.

"Yeah, I guess so."

Susan began to stand and I pulled her hand back down. "Susan, wait. I'm really, really sorry. For tonight"—I paused, rubbing her hand with my thumb—"and everything."

She smiled, leaning in to kiss my cheek. "Thanks, Michael. Does this mean I'm not a bitch?"

I put my arms on her shoulders as she stood, and looked into her eyes. "Not even close!"

"Cool, I'm trying to move away from that role, ha!"

"And you are. Keep on going. I've got you in my prayers."

"Thanks, I'm gonna need all the prayers I can get."

She smiled as we parted, and I sat back down, watching her car pull away and taking a few deep breaths to calm down. *This sure could have been a lot worse. Thank God Susan wasn't drinking. I wonder why she left the program and went to Harry's. That's pretty wild. I should get Nick up to bed so he can get a good night's rest, although judging by the smell coming from his breath, he'd probably sleep well on a bed of nails.*

I'd risen and started toward the door when approaching headlights got my attention. A white Jeep rolled to a stop at the curb. I watched as the driver turned off the engine and came around the front of the vehicle. Jackie looked beautiful in the pale streetlight as her cowboy boots clicked up the walkway toward me. I stepped off the porch step and she stopped in front of me.

"Hey, you OK?" she asked.

I nodded, trying to make sense of why she was here, not that I wasn't happy to see her. "Yeah, yeah, I'm fine. Just been a crazy-ass day."

She stepped in, putting her arms around my neck. My arms wrapped easily around her familiar waist. I took in her smell and my shoulders relaxed as our hips squeezed together. "It's OK," she whispered. "It's OK." We stayed that way for some time. It felt nice.

I told Jackie I was gonna get Nick up to his bed, and she followed to help. He woke slightly when I roused him from the couch and kept mumbling about how "she wasn't getting any better" and "I think I'll die without her." He managed to walk up the stairs with a lot of help. I helped him pull off his jeans and he collapsed into bed, quickly assuming a fetal position. I couldn't help but think about his young child in

Anna's womb in the same position. Staring down at Nick, an idea came to me. One that I'd act on tomorrow.

Jackie covered him with a blanket, then we made our way downstairs.

"I think he's gonna be fine. Probably will have a huge headache in the morning," I said.

"Yep," she said. "I think so."

"So how'd you know I was here?"

"Susan texted me when she was leaving Harry's with Nick. She said you were out of town, and I thought maybe I could help her if she needed it, so I changed my plans and got here as soon as I could."

I nodded. "Got it. I was really worried at first, 'cause Jesse said she'd been drinking. But she hadn't. She was great tonight. She left just a few minutes before you got here."

"I know, she's doing good; I'm really proud of her."

I nodded as we stood leaning against the kitchen counters across from each other.

She looked to the floor, then to me. "I'm gonna get going." She paused, looking intently at me. "You want to come over?"

I paused, suppressing the "yes" that instantly rose in my throat. "What about Jon?"

"It's OK, he's out of town. And I'm not sure about us anyway. We're not really . . . exclusive. And Nick doesn't really need you. He'll just sleep it off. You could just leave him a note to call you in the morning."

She walked to me and placed her arms around my neck and her mouth next to my ear. "You've had a really long and stressful day. Just come over and relax." We talked another minute, before I grabbed a pen and paper from the counter and scribbled a quick note to Nick. A minute later I was opening the door of her Jeep.

I awoke the next morning, instantly aware of the softness of the sheets; thread count is what I've been told it is. I took a deep breath and opened my eyes to the unfamiliar surroundings of Anna and Nick's guest room. The mocha-colored walls caught the early morning sun. The sound of coughing coming from the hallway announced Nick's arrival at the door. He was holding the note I'd written him before I'd walked Jackie to her Jeep.

He stood there in his underwear, hair a mess, and began to talk in a scratchy and hung-over voice.

"So I found this on the floor next to my bed. What does *Come see me in the guest room when you wake up and you can thank me* mean? What happened last night? I don't remember much of it."

I laughed, throwing a pillow at him. He collapsed on the floor next to the bed. He propped his head on the pillow, and let out a deep breath. "Please tell me I didn't do anything stupid."

I leaned over the side. "Hey, buddy, no, you're all good. I came back to town and missed you at Harry's. I knew Susan was there and I was thinking the worst, but she got you out of the bar and back here. She was just leaving when I got here. Nothing happened." I paused as he took a deep breath, staring at the ceiling. "I know you're hurting, Nick, and we'll get this figured out, trust me."

"Damn, that's right. Susan," he said. "She brought me home?"

I nodded. "Yep, but she wasn't drinking and she tucked you in on the couch." I filled Nick in on the rest of what had happened, leaving out the late-night visit from Jackie, as I just didn't have the energy to get into it. I told Nick to take a shower while I fixed breakfast, then I'd drive his car to the hospital.

An hour later, we were nearing the hospital. Nick told me to pull the car to the curb in front of the drop off area. I put the car in park and turned to him. "What's up?"

He stared out the window as he began. "Michael, I almost screwed up last night. I mean . . ."

I interrupted, "Come on Nick."

He shut me down. "No, just be quiet. Listen to me. Somebody suggested I stop by Harry's for a beer or two and some of the game, but what the f—. What was I thinking?" His voice rose. "This is not good, Anna's not good, and the baby's not good. I'm a strong guy, with a strong faith. And I know this sounds like I'm playing the victim"—he turned to me—"but something good has got to happen soon. Hour after hour, I just sit there watching Anna, expecting her to wake up at any minute. And it doesn't happen, and doesn't happen. And I don't know what's happening with her, if she's in pain and if the baby is OK. Honestly, Michael, there are times I'm not sure I can stay there and be with her, be the strong person she's expecting me to be. I don't want to feel this way, but I do, and I'm scared."

"I know this is hard, Nick. Anyone in your position would be stressed out." For some reason I thought about something I'd learned when I was in the pros. "When I was playing ball, there were a lot of times when the work was hard or monotonous or I was trying to recover from an injury. I was taught to imagine the positive outcome I was looking for, be it the combines right after high school and college, a big game, or even just a workout. And it helped me stay positive. Maybe the same will help you. Imagine it's a year from now and you're home with Anna and your baby. Focus on that vision. The guy who taught me that always said we have to hold useful thoughts."

I turned my head and saw he had his eyes closed. After a few minutes, he opened them. He looked a little calmer.

"Thanks, buddy. You going to come up?"

"Not right now. There's something I have to do. But I'll be back as soon as I can."

After a quick trip home to check in with my mom and tell her about my ill-fated brush with fame and glory in New York, I jumped into Nick's car and headed to the place I knew I had to go, Brew Ha Ha. My intuition was telling me that I'd find Jay there—I had to.

CHAPTER 15

The Fear

With men this is impossible, but with God all things are possible. - Jesus of Nazareth

I pulled into the lot, smiling as I passed Jay's Camaro backed into a spot, gleaming like a kid's bike under the Christmas tree. I parked and walked toward the coffee shop, noticing another familiar car.

The shop was busy as staff scurried around with trays of steaming mugs, acai bowls and huge muffins. The same mother I'd seen Jay help before was in a chair in the corner, scrolling away on her iPhone, as her brown-haired, healthy cherub sat in the stroller next to her, wearing the smallest Nikes I'd ever seen, and fully engaged with the bustling environment.

Sheila saw me first and waved me over. I made my way to the old wooden table, thankful for her welcoming embrace. "Michael! It's great to see you here. I'm really, really sorry about the New York thing. You would've been great. But I think it's special that you put your friends ahead of the job." She stopped speaking and gestured to the man sitting across from her. "I want you to meet my friend I've been telling you about."

I turned from Sheila to Jay, who had stood up and smiled.

Jay spoke first. "Hello, Michael, nice to see you again. Join us for coffee?"

Sheila pursed her lips, turning her head to the side. "Wait, you know each other?

I gave Jay a high-five, winking at Sheila, "Yes, we know each other."

"But wait, how? Why didn't I know?" We sat and I ordered a coffee and yogurt parfait with extra granola from our server.

I looked to Jay. "You want this?"

"No, it's all yours." He chuckled.

Sheila sat back. "Oh, this ought to be good.

"Well," I said, taking a sip of my coffee. "Jay and I—it is Jay, right?" He nodded with a smile. "We met in Harry's one night when I was in there with Jackie, so it must have been shortly after I came back home. And we've met a few other times since then." I looked to Sheila. "But those are stories for another time." I turned to Jay. "And I really appreciated your text yesterday. Thanks for keeping Anna in your prayers, she sure needs them." He nodded again as he put his mug to his lips.

Sheila crossed her legs and sat back in her wooden chair. She wore a loose T-shirt with the letters dldsm on the front. "So this is wild. I can see now that while I've been telling each of you about each other, I never mentioned names, or who you each were." She was smiling. "How cool. I love this kind of stuff."

I agreed. "Yes, it is. Actually, when we talked yesterday and you said I needed to meet your friend Jay, I thought that maybe it was you." I turned to Jay. "So, yes, this is cool."

I pointed my spoon at Sheila's T-shirt. "What's *d-l-d-s-m* stand for?"

Sheila looked to Jay. "Jay gave it to me. It's a T-shirt line that his friend Brendan has." She leaned closer so I could see the small words in parenthesis under the larger five letters.

I read it out loud, laughing when I got to the end. "Don't let dumb sh*t matter."

"And check out the back." She stood and turned around, showing me a logo with the letters jckrbbt and a rabbit jumping over the bbt. "Brendan is a writer and speaker who gives proceeds from these shirts to an organization that supports people in recovery from addiction to drugs and alcohol, and another that supports families in getting back on their feet with housing when they've fallen on bad times."

"Two great causes. I'll have to get a few." I looked to Jay.

"We can make that happen," he said. "Sheila and I had a great meditation practice this morning, didn't we?" She nodded, then Jay continued, "I really wish more people would practice the principle of being still. There's so much in there. We offered our practice to Anna, sending her prayers and healing energy. It's kind of like people are all running around, stressed and overwhelmed and yelling for relief, yet they do nothing to produce some calm. A teacher of mine once said it's like they're standing knee deep in a river and dying of thirst."

Sheila and I laughed, as I replied, "That sure is right."

"There's an energy in stillness that most people leave on the table; they don't develop habits of stillness, and they continue to struggle for answers way more than they have to," he said. He looked out the window and spoke slowly. "It's often in the absence of sound that we hear the most."

There was a pause as that statement sank in. Sheila broke the stillness by springing to her feet. "Well, I would love to sit here in the coffee shop all day and talk philosophy. But I've got to get home and shower and get to work, or I'm gonna have a lot of time to be still without a job."

Jay and I rose, saying our goodbyes. "OK, you boys have fun. See you later." She turned to me. "I'm gonna head over to the hospital to see Anna later tonight after work. I hope she has a better day. Maybe see you there?"

"Yep, I'll be there."

"OK, have a great day." She turned back over her shoulder. "Luv you guys."

Jay stood. "I'm going to get a refill. Do you want one?"

"No, I'm good," I replied with a nervous smile. *Calm down, it's all gonna be OK. When he comes back, you're gonna tell him you need to talk to him. And don't beat around the bush, just come out with it.* I switched seats so I would be next to Jay and not across from him, though I wasn't sure that would be an advantage. I noticed the empty tables around us as I tried to get some moisture into my mouth and repeatedly wiped my sweaty palms on my jeans.

Jay returned and sat down. "So what's on your agenda for today?"

I took a quick look out the window to see a man drop his cup of coffee in the parking lot, then make some angry gestures as he looked at his splattered pants. "I need to ask you something. Sort of a favor."

Jay looked into my eyes. "Yes, I know."

Flustered, I shook my head and leaned back in my chair. "What do you mean you know?"

He smiled softly, tilting his head at me and allowing me time to remember who I was talking with, something that was not fully absorbed by my psyche yet. "Oh, yeah, yeah, right," I said at last. "Of course you do. Sorry."

He shook his head then sipped from his bright blue mug. "No apology needed. I get it. It happens almost every time I visit someone here. The others have told me they experience the same thing." *Others? I thought. What does he mean by others?*

Jay looked to the door as a few teenage girls walked in, phones in hand. "You want me to cure Anna and make sure the baby will be born healthy. Then this nightmare will be in the rearview mirror of life's journey for you and your friends."

I stayed quiet in spite of the urge to say something. *Shit, how does he know? I mean I know how he knows, but . . . OK, just breathe. Breathe.* Finally, I spoke. "Yes. Yes, I do." I wanted to give him all the reasons why, but couldn't say more.

Our gazes met and we remained that way for a minute until a smile spread across his face. He replied simply, "OK."

I grabbed his hand. "Really? You mean it? Thank you, Jay, thank you. I know there are a lot of people in the world suffering even more than Nick and Anna are . . . but they're such good people, and this will mean so much. . . ." My voice trailed off.

"Calm down, Michael. I know you love these three people—baby included, of course—but this is not about suffering. Let me offer you something to consider. While we're here as humans, we suffer, some of us much more often and longer than others. Our suffering is not a controlled thing; it's just part of life. What is controlled is that I"—he paused, then continued with a new emphasis—"we will, sometimes, protect people from suffering, or give them the strength to bear it." He looked away. A sense of peace had risen within me when he said we.

"So how does this work? Do you have to do that laying-on-of-hands thing? Could we . . . um, you . . . do it tonight? We could go to the hospital. I'll be lookout, you know, make sure no one will see us. Especially that nurse, Audrey. She's a tough one. She's the swing shift nurse and she's a good one. She's on top of things there." I chuckled. "Although I'm not sure if she ever sleeps. She kind of reminds me of a nun Nick and I had back in grade school."

Jay stopped my babbling. "Yes, I've seen my share of nuns who needed more sleep." He drained his mug, and stood. "Listen, Michael, tonight is good. I've got to go now, but I'll text you when I get to the hospital. Sound good?"

I stood. "Yeah, yeah, sounds good. I'm going to head over there right after dinner, so I'll be there ready to keep a lookout. I'll try to get anyone around there to maybe go home for the night. so there are fewer people around. If I can't get Nick to go home, I'll try to get him to take a nap while I sit with Anna."

Once again, Jay stopped my babbling. He took my right hand in his, and placed his left hand on my shoulder. "Michael, trust me, it doesn't matter who's there; they will not see us."

"OK, right, we'll be careful."

"Michael, you're not getting it, my friend. They will not see us." He gave me a wink and left Brew Ha Ha. I watched him walk to his Camaro, then he stopped and looked back at me through the glass. He said nothing, just smiled, and I heard his voice in my head. "And Michael, this is just between us, right?" His smile grew as I held up my right thumb. I shook my head at what had just happened. The now-familiar words continued to thrum in my brain: *Wow. This is crazy.*

I drove Nick's car over to the hospital and spent a few hours there as I'd promised Nick I would. He said there'd been no change in Anna, but he sensed something bad was going to happen or was happening. "They're all just acting a little weird," he'd said about the nurses and doctors.

Mom came to pick me up, and we grabbed a late lunch. I spent the rest of the day doing errands and trying to reach Tara to see if I'd really blown my chance at TV stardom.

Throughout the day, my focus—my thoughts—were on the night and what was going to happen.

About 7 o'clock I grabbed a quick shower. My mom had gone to dinner with some friends and I'd told her I might be home later or might sleep at the hospital. As I walked to my Jeep, I saw it was a clear night. Looking at the bright stars provided some brief reprieve from my nervousness. I'm not sure why, but I took a drive past Jay's house on the way, and was surprised not to see his car in the driveway. *What does he do with his time? I wonder what he's doing now.*

I pulled into the parking garage at the hospital and moved quickly toward the ICU. On my walk I noticed all the hospital staff moving around, and the image of Jay and me getting caught hijacked my thoughts. It was all I could think about. *What was I thinking asking Jay to do this? I'm gonna text him and call it off.*

> Hey Jay. I just got to the hospital. Lots of people around. Let's not do anything tonight. Don't come here. I'll text you later and let you know how Anna's doing.

"Good evening, Michael," a woman's voice said. I looked up and realized I'd made it to the ICU, not remembering much of the trip.

I slipped my phone in the back pocket of my jeans. "Oh, hi, Audrey. Sorry about that. I didn't mean to be rude, I just got caught up in a text I was sending."

"Oh, no problem." She shook her head. "Most people who walk by me have their head down looking at their phones." I felt my phone vibrate, alerting me that a text had come in. I guessed it was from Jay. "Anna is still fighting, but . . ." Audrey paused.

"But what?" I asked.

Audrey looked sad. "But nothing. She's going to be OK."

"Let's hope so," I said out of habit.

She placed some papers in a tray on her desk and looked at me. "Michael, I believe our words have energy, and I don't do the 'hope' thing. That just feels to me that we're wishing somebody else will do something, that we're not using our own strength. Kind of like we've got some energy we can use and we don't even know it. When we *hope*, it seems to me we turn things over to chance."

I was surprised by Audrey's response and a bit confused by her philosophizing. My curiosity got the best of me. "If not hope, then what?"

She stood and came around the desk, carrying an iPad. "I *trust*, Michael. *Trust*. I'm not hoping Anna is going to make it through this critical time, I'm trusting." She nodded and moved in quick choppy steps into a room behind us.

I grabbed my phone, unlocked the screen, and looked at the text, from Jay as I'd suspected. His response made the hair on the back of my neck stand up, and my legs weak. I leaned on Audrey's nurses' station.

Trust. Just trust.

"You OK?" Audrey asked as she came back to her station, taking a seat. "You look a little pale."

I ran my hands through my hair, and headed toward Anna's room. "Yes, I'm OK." I'm pretty sure she didn't hear the other two words I whispered to myself. "I think."

Nick sat in the lounge down the hall, with both sets of parents and some other friends and family. He was clean-shaven, and his eyes looked much clearer. He told me Sheila would be over later, and then left to go sit with Anna.

Nick's mom came to me and said, "Let's take a walk, Michael." I'd known this woman for most of my life and thought of her as my "other mother." "How about a cup of coffee? Or a hot chocolate?"

"Sounds good." We left the lounge and headed to the cafeteria and vending machines, which were down a few floors.

Hot chocolates in hand, we sat near a small fountain in the lobby outside the cafeteria. Her hair was more disheveled than the last time I'd seen her, and her eyes lacked the usual makeup and the sparkle I'd seen so many times. "Michael, Anna's not good, and it seems to be getting worse. The doctors have been in and out all day long, and while they're talking with us, I feel like they're not really talking to us. Does that make sense?"

"Yes, that's the same thing Nick said this morning."

She looked at me, tears in her eyes. "I hate to see what this is doing to him. He's not doing very well, not very well at all. You know I love Anna and am praying hard for her—and our grandchild. But I'm a mess thinking about Nick. He's so distant. I've never seen him this way, he's always been so strong and optimistic." I put my hand on her shoulder as she began to cry.

"It's gonna be OK, Mrs. Watley. We just have to trust. We just have to trust."

We went back to the lounge on Anna's floor. Nick's mom went to sit with his dad. Anna's parents were still there too. A younger woman sat in the corner, sipping from a water bottle and thumbing away on her phone. She was dressed in all white—pants, T-shirt, sneakers and ski jacket. Her blond hair hung down in soft curls. I tried to determine her age but she was one of those people who could have been 28 or 40.

A moment later Anna's dad came to me, his face ashen, his eyes red and moist. "We're going to head home now and get some rest, Michael. Thanks for being here with Nick. We'll see you tomorrow." I could not even imagine what this man and all these people were feeling inside their hearts. The pain of watching your child suffer must be among the worst possible type.

"All right, I'll come back tomorrow, too. I'm sure something positive will happen soon and Anna will turn the corner." We exchanged goodbyes. Nick's parents left a few minutes later, leaving only me and the woman in white. I felt so alone. My phone buzzed; it was Jay, and his text asked me to meet him at the window seat just outside the ICU doors. The woman in the lounge looked up as I let out my breath with a loud whooshing noise. "Sorry," I said. She smiled slightly and turned her focus back to her phone.

I arrived at the window seat. A few magazines were scattered on the cushions. I grabbed them as I sat, placing them farther back on the seat next to the glass.

"Hey, Michael." I turned at the voice and saw Sheila coming out of the ICU doors. She was crying. I'd forgotten she was coming over.

"Oh, hey, Sheila. What's going on?" I jumped as I felt a finger poke my shoulder and turned, nearly letting out a scream at the sight of Jay sitting next to me on the window seat. Just then I felt Sheila lean in on my shoulders, give me a hug, and kiss my cheek before she pulled away.

"I just had an awful conversation with Nick. I'd heard the nurses talking about how the doctors didn't see any progress in Anna, and being a nurse, I knew what they were saying." She fought back tears. "Michael, I know I talked a lot about how everything was going to be OK, but now . . . after what I heard, it's quite possible she may never get better. It's maybe too dangerous to bring her out of the medically induced coma . . . and, well, I tried to talk to Nick about preparing for the worst, but let's just say he didn't want to hear it."

I stood to get away from Jay, who was leaning back against the pillow in the window seat, legs crossed. Sheila looked at me quizzically. "You OK? You seem a little nervous."

Man, she can't see him. He was right. This is getting stranger by the minute. "Yeah, yeah, I'm fine. Just got a lot on my mind," I stammered.

She plopped down on the bench, right where Jay had been sitting. In fact, she'd gone right through him. I felt ill.

"Nick threw me out of the room," Sheila continued. "And I feel so bad about trying to confront him that way. I just thought it would be harder in the end if he doesn't deal with reality."

I sat down on the bench, as far away from Jay as possible, and took Sheila's hands. "It's OK, Sheila. We're all very stressed right now," I said.

"Are you going to see them?" she asked.

"In a few minutes."

"Tell Nick I'm sorry . . . that . . . that I just gave in to despair for a moment. I didn't mean to make things harder on him."

"I know you were trying to help," I replied. "I'm sure Nick will forgive you." I stood. "Let me walk you to your car, OK?"

When I got back, I found Jay sitting on that same bench outside the ICU door. He was cross-legged in the window seat, eyes closed, hands in his lap, breathing slowly.

I sat next to him, took a deep breath, and closed my eyes as well. I began to say a few prayers, as my mind raced in between. *This is funny in a way, I guess. Here I am praying for my friends and Jay . . . is right next to me. Maybe I should just talk with him, pray to him, with him.*

Jay's voice pulled me from my thoughts. "You ready?"

My elbows rested on my thighs, my head in my hands. I ran my fingers through my hair. "Yes. I guess."

"No guessing. Just commit . . . and trust. Remember?"

"Yeah, I remember, Jay, but give me a little break here. I kinda feel like I'm living in the Twilight Zone at the moment. Didn't you hear Sheila?" My voice was laced with anger and frustration. "Didn't you hear what she said?"

Jay began talking without looking at me. "I did hear Sheila, and she's right, things are not good. But Michael, remember, all things are possible. Deep down inside you know it or you wouldn't have asked me to come here tonight." He paused. "I'll leave if you'd like, and maybe we can come back another time."

My head hurt, and the thoughts swirled as sweat soaked into my shirt. I tried to talk in spite of my mouth feeling like it was stuffed with cotton. "No, no, we're here. Another time may be too late. I want to make something positive happen for Anna."

Jay turned to me, his voice peaceful. "Then you need to get to that deep place inside you . . . in your soul, that knows this is possible."

I began to speak but jumped back as the ICU doors opened and Nick walked toward us. He was looking at us . . . or maybe through us is a better phrase. "Don't worry," Jay said. "He can't see or hear us, Michael." Nick walked by, his breathing shallow, and his eyes and hair a mess.

"OK, good," I said. "I'm glad he didn't see us. Nobody will be able to, right?"

Jay shook his head. "Not unless you want them to. Look, we're good. Don't think about it anymore. We can do the Harry Potter invisibility cloak thing if that will make you feel better." He chuckled quietly, relieving a bit of my panic.

"Nope." I put my arm around his shoulder. "We're good. Let's go."

We walked in silence past Audrey, focused on her iPad, and another nurse eating some yogurt. Jay got to Anna's door first, stepped aside and motioned for me to go in. I put my hand on the door and pushed gently. The door swung in, and I immediately saw Anna's bandaged head, the tubes running from both her arms. The one coming from her mouth was fixed in place with white medical tape. The machines sucked and dinged and hissed, creating an absurd-sounding orchestra. The reality of our situation hit me, and I turned to Jay, who I'm sure saw the fear and doubt in my eyes. He placed his hand on my shoulder as he slid past me to Anna's bedside.

Jay moved his hand toward Anna but pulled it back slowly as the door opened and Nick entered, sipping through a straw from a paper cup in one hand and holding a bag of popcorn in the other. He walked to the corner chair and collapsed into it, spilling some of the popcorn onto the floor. I stared at him and he seemed to be looking right at me, right through me. After a few handfuls of popcorn, crumbs now dotting his dark shirt, he placed the cup on the table and closed his eyes.

Again, Jay began reaching his hand toward Anna, but then he stopped, pulled his hand back, and turned to me with a whisper. "You do it."

I looked to Anna, then to Jay, then back to Anna, wiping the sweat from my forehead and resisting with all my might the desire to run out of the room. "What, me? No way! Are you crazy?" His eyes looked into mine; he said nothing. After a few seconds, I said softly, "Me? Can I?"

Jay paused, then said softly. "Say those two words again, but reverse them and no need for the question mark."

I paused, squinting and trying to get my thoughts around what Jay was suggesting. Slowly, quietly I spoke. "I can."

Jay's eyes were locked on mine, his face peaceful. "Say it again."

"I can."

"Yes, Michael, you can."

I paused, grounding myself in the moment and convincing myself about what was happening. "Yes, if I just trust and believe in you."

"Not exactly," Jay whispered. My eyes narrowed and my head tilted. "There are millions and millions who believe in me. What's needed is for them to believe in the me that is in them. Michael, believe in me . . . in you."

Silence settled. I'm not sure how long; I was lost in the enormity of the moment. I wiped my palms on my pants. My head throbbed. As I turned to look at Jay, my peripheral vision caught Anna's eyes as they opened and she looked toward us. I was unsure if she'd scream or make a noise, but she just smiled the smallest smile possible. She nodded slightly to me as if to say, "It's OK. I believe you can do this."

My mind raced with doubt and confusion, my shirt and forehead now bathed in sweat. Anna tried to speak through the breathing tube and medical tape across her lips. I shook my head at her, wanting her to remain still but at the same time frustrated that I couldn't hear her. Then, in the quiet, I caught her voice. "Thank you." She seemed to take a deep breath in spite of the breathing tube, then closed her eyes.

I looked to Jay, shaking my head. "Did you hear her? Did you? She said, 'Thank you.' "

"Yes," he said softly. "I heard. Let Anna's gratitude be the energy that you need—along with your faith."

I closed my eyes and searched out the stillness. I thought about everything I'd been through in the past months, about what Anna and Nick had been through. I thought about how badly I wanted to help them and the baby that was growing in Anna's womb. I thought about Jay's faith in me and my faith in him. And I thought about the divine that was inside me and all around me.

I pulled my right hand from my side, moving it toward Anna until it hovered inches above her heart. Intense heat filled my hand. I stayed like that, my thoughts not really thoughts at all but more a conscious energy that I was channeling to Anna. Time was no longer relevant.

My body surged and my heart started pounding and beating faster than it ever had. And then it slowed quickly, settling into an easy rhythm. I took a deep breath and opened my eyes. I looked to Jay, who smiled at me then nodded to Anna. Her eyes opened slightly and she tried to smile through the breathing tube. The gray color in her cheeks was replaced by a warm pink tone that enveloped her entire face. A bright light rose from her entire body and she took one more peaceful breath as her eyes closed and her right hand moved slowly to rest on her stomach. Nick stirred in his chair as we left the room.

CHAPTER 16

The Riddle

Faith is simply belief without proof.

The rest of the night was a total blur. I remember walking out of Anna's room with Jay, my body trembling. We passed Audrey's desk. She stopped what she was doing and looked up, but seemed to look right through us just as Nick had done. I walked with Jay through the ICU doors. He gave me a hug and headed to the elevators. I saw the young woman from earlier asleep on a couch, blond hair peeking out from under her white North Face jacket. *I wonder who she's here for.*

I returned to the bench outside the ICU doors, feeling completely exhausted. I closed my eyes but sleep eluded me; the energy from what had happened lingered in a tingling sensation throughout my body.

I guess I finally drifted off, and was awakened as the sun came through the parted curtains, the weak rays still managing to warm my face. I was startled to see Nick coming through the doors toward me. His face broke into a huge smile. I stood and walked to meet him.

"Hey, buddy, you OK?"

His grin grew even larger, if that was possible. "She's awake."

I rubbed my eyes. "What?" As I stood, I saw the young blond woman from the lounge walk past us, through the ICU doors. Nick didn't seem to notice her.

"She's awake, Michael. Anna's awake."

He grabbed my arm, pulling me through the doors and back toward Anna's room. A nurse I didn't know came out of a patient's room, and Nick yelled, "Nurse! I need your help! Come over here . . . fast."

Her pace quickened and her voice was nervous. "What's the matter? Is it Anna? Is she OK?"

Nick smiled, "Yes, it's Anna. She's awake!"

"What?" the nurse said over her shoulder as she moved to the room. "This is not possible."

Upon entering Anna's room, I saw the nurse fiddling with a tube hanging from one of the machines. I heard her say "Sweet Jesus" under her breath as she turned to see Nick holding Anna's hand.

The nurse moved to Anna. "Anna dear, can you hear me?" Anna nodded slightly. "Are you in pain?" Anna moved her head from side to side in a motion that I could have missed had I not just heard the nurse's prompt. "This is crazy, she should still be in the coma." She saw that the drip bag was empty. "There's no way all the medication could have been discharged. This is just crazy." The nurse made her way quickly to the door as she barked an order. "You two stay here with her. I need to get the doctor."

Nick leaned in and kissed Anna, "Oh my God, honey, I knew you'd be back, I just prayed and prayed." She smiled, then slowly turned her gaze to me. Our eyes connected and we both silently acknowledged what had happened.

We stayed with Anna until Dr. Ali came in. He looked at Anna briefly, then went to focus on a few monitors and pumps, pressing buttons and looking through the changing screens. He asked us to leave, sounding nervous. Nick and I moved to the lounge. "I gotta call our parents," he said. "And why don't you call Sheila."

"Yep, good idea." I was leaving a voicemail for Sheila when I heard Nick scream into the phone enthusiastically, "Mom, listen to me. I don't know what happened. All I know is she's awake and you all need to get down here now."

Nick hit the phone screen, slipped the device into his pocket and gave me a long, tight hug. "I just can't believe it, I can't believe it. Did you see how good she looks? I mean her eyes, and her color. Oh man, I gotta hear what the doctor says."

"Well, here he comes." We turned to see Dr. Ali walking quickly our way.

He spoke to Nick. "We need to run some tests on Anna, Nick. This is very confusing. It will take a few hours and then I want to talk with you and all the parents."

He'd begun to turn when Nick grabbed the arm of his white coat. "Dr. Ali," he said, "this is good, right?"

The doctor pursed his lips and squinted. "It sure looks that way, but frankly I'm not sure what to think. I'm going to call Dr. Chelson, run some tests, and get some scans. We'll talk after that."

When the parents showed up with coffee, doughnuts, smiles and an energy that had lain dormant these past few weeks, we all gathered in the lounge. They were all disappointed that Anna had been rolled away for testing and hung on every word as Nick and I recounted the early-morning events. "I just knew she was a fighter," Anna's dad got out through his tears. "She always has been."

It seemed odd to me that no one asked about the baby. I guess maybe in their subconscious they just wanted to stay in tune with the good news . . . or at least what seemed like good news.

I had texted Jay but had not heard back, and Sheila arrived not long after the parents and said that she was surprised that Jay had not been in her meditation class that morning. Hmmm, I thought, *I wonder what's up.*

A few minutes after 11 o'clock, Dr. Chelson came through the ICU doors, her face lacking any particular emotion. Pleasantries were exchanged, and Dr. Chelson invited Nick and the parents to a conference room down the hall for a meeting with her and Dr. Ali.

"Dr. Chelson, we need to have Sheila and Michael there too," Nick said. "They have to come. They're like family." She nodded. "And everything's good with Anna, right, Doctor?"

She turned. "Nick, let's just talk about it in a few minutes."

Both doctors were seated at the table when we all came into the room. Dr. Ali stood and shook hands with Nick and his father. Nick sat across from Dr. Chelson, his mom next to him and his dad standing behind him with his hand on Nick's shoulder. Dr. Chelson started in. "We have some news about Anna. I'd like for Dr. Ali to let you know what the tests revealed."

Nick turned to the man. "I'm not sure what's going on here, but all I know is Anna was awake this morning and she looked good. So why do you both look like you're going to tell us something bad?"

Dr. Ali walked to the wall and turned on a light on the side of a screen, revealing what looked to be a few X-rays of a skull. "Nick, we do have some news, and we're confused. I've never seen this before in all my years practicing medicine. You know the other day after Anna's surgery when you asked about the baby?" Nick nodded. "And you'll recall that I said this would be much better for the baby if it was a year from now and Anna was healed after the surgery."

"Sure, Dr. Ali, I remember." Nick locked his fingers behind his head. "Something's wrong with the baby, right?" Anna's mom started to cry, making sniffling noises and wiping her eyes with a napkin.

Dr. Ali pulled a pen from his jacket breast pocket and pointed to the X-ray. "Nick, this is Anna's brain just after the surgery, and you can see from this area that it was damaged, and right here is the swelling we were concerned about."

"Yeah, OK," Nick said, his eyes not leaving the X-ray.

"Here"—Dr. Ali used his pen as a pointer, referencing another film—"is the same area from the scan we did this morning." Dr. Ali looked to Dr. Chelson, who just nodded.

"So what? It looks a lot different. Isn't that good?"

"Dr. Chelson and I are confused, because this brain scan from this morning is one that we should be seeing a year from now, not after only two days." Anna's mom gasped and she put her hand over her mouth.

It was Nick who was crying now. Through his tears, he stammered, "So, she's gonna be alright, she's OK?"

"Yes, it appears that way."

"And the baby?" Nick asked.

Dr. Chelson looked right at Nick. "We'll have to see. The baby is stable, but right now we need to focus on Anna and get her stronger and not have any more treatments for the time being."

For some reason, my stomach was upset and I felt lightheaded. Sheila and I exchanged glances. I excused myself and entered the hallway, looking down toward Anna's room. I froze as I saw the young woman in the white ski jacket enter her room. I hurried to the room, opening the door quickly. The woman was standing next to Anna. She turned to me and smiled, then placed her hand on Anna's belly. Anna's eyes were closed above the smile on her face; her breathing was slow and peaceful. A bright light glowed outward from the woman's body for a few seconds. Then she just disappeared. She was there and then gone.

I realized I was holding my breath, and let it out. Anna's eyes remained closed as a few machines continued to make their noises. I left the room and went to the nurses' station.

"Amazing news about Anna," the nurse said. I made no reply. She looked at me. "Are you OK, sir?"

"Yes, yes, I'm OK. And yes, great news." I paused. "Excuse me, but did you see that young woman who just walked past? The one who in the lounge last night wearing the white jacket? Was she here to visit a family member?"

The nurse tilted her head, a confused look on her face. "I'm sorry, sir, but I don't know what you're talking about. Anna's family were the only ones here last night and this morning, except for an older couple in to see a woman down the hall. But they were here earlier." I smiled and walked through the metal doors to get some air outside, feeling in my gut that I'd expected her to say that.

CHAPTER 17

The Healing

Always remember the wonderful possibility
and potential that lies in one's future.

A few days later, Mom and I went out for breakfast. I was still distracted, my mind holding onto thoughts of Tuesday's events and the woman in white. *I think I know what it was all about.*

Mom and I ordered our favorite omelets. As she finished stirring her tea, she glanced up, giving me a peculiar look.

"What?" I said.

"What *what*?" she replied through a crooked smile. I shook my head and she continued. "I'm just so happy about Anna, it really is something else. I know she is a strong young woman, but the doctors don't seem to know what's going on, and traditional medicine sure doesn't seem to explain anything. It seems like a miracle, doesn't it?"

"I agree. Nick and his parents are doing so much better. I was really, really worried about Nick." I paused. "It was difficult to watch my best friend, and a really stable person . . . on the verge of losing it. I was scared."

"I know you were, honey. I know a lot happened this fall—with getting cut, trying to find a new path in life, and Anna and Nick. But I must say it seems you've changed." She wore a small, thoughtful smile.

"What do you mean? I'm probably out of pro ball for good. I blew my TV chance. I still don't have a job. It seems like me and Jackie are over for good, though I'm pretty sure I'll always love her." I took a sip of coffee. "But maybe it's just that I'm beginning to love her in a different way."

My mom shook her head. "Yes, yes, I know all that. I just don't know how to describe it, but you just seem different to me, more peaceful . . . if that makes sense."

I'm not sure what Mom's trying to say here, but I guess I get it. I guess I was really letting the stress of life get to me. "Yep, that makes a lot of sense, Mom." We finished our breakfast, and she insisted on treating me, as she always did. "And at least I have my own house now." Mom just smiled, holding up her right thumb in a show of support.

Late that afternoon, I pulled into the hospital lot, quickly finding a parking spot. As I was about to open the car door, I heard my phone buzz. It was a text from Tara.

> Mr. Heisman Trophy really bombed in his latest test.
> Have convinced my bosses to give you another chance.
> RSVP ASAP if interested.

I couldn't type fast enough.

> Yes! Can be there Monday at 7 am. Good?

She responded right away, agreeing to the time. *Guess I didn't blow my chance after all.*

I grabbed the two bunches of fresh flowers from my back seat and headed up to the ICU, predictably in a great frame of mind.

When I was almost there, I remembered that Nick had said Anna might be moved to a different floor today, but I was close enough that I decided to just check in at the ICU.

As I walked toward Anna's room, I sensed someone behind me and turned to see Audrey, who had just come from a patient's room.

"Happy Friday afternoon, Michael. How are you?"

I turned and slowed, allowing Audrey to walk next to me. "I'm doing good, Audrey. How about you?"

She placed her tablet on the desk at the nurses' station. "All good here, thankfully not real busy, which is a good thing. But I've got to tell you it was with mixed emotions that we got Anna out of here a few hours ago. She is doing so well and looking great, and the baby seems stronger as well."

"That was my next question. She's on a different floor?"

"Yep, sixth floor, Room 611." She winked at me. "And can you believe she was lucky enough to get a private room?"

I put my arm around her shoulders. "Oh, now, let me see how that might have happened." We both laughed as I handed her a bunch of the flowers, leaning in to kiss her cheek. "Audrey, thanks for everything you've done for Anna, and all of us. You sure are a special lady." She took the flowers with sparkling eyes. I walked down the hall, out the ICU doors for what I was trusting would be the last time.

The bell dinged as the number 6 lit up on the elevator panel. The doors opened and I made a quick left toward Room 611.

"Oh, well, hello, Michael," Nick's mom said as I bumped into her and the others. "How are you? I see you found out they moved Anna."

"Yep. Just saw the wonderful Audrey and she pointed me in this direction. Where are you all off to?"

Anna's mom came to me and grabbed my arm. "Can I assume these flowers are for the two of us?" She laughed as she nodded to Nick's mom.

We all laughed. "Oh, uh, no. These are for Anna. Um, I have yours in my car."

"Oh, sure you do," she said, as I became aware of the warmth I felt from these people smiling and laughing again and looking more like themselves. *Funny how the stress of suffering can have an impact on us physically as well as emotionally.* "We're heading down the street to get a bite to eat. Nick went a few minutes ago to get us a table. You'll come join us, right?" The others agreed with the invitation.

"I'd love to, but I really want to spend some time with Anna. Can I go in? Is she awake?"

Anna's dad chimed in, "Yeah, sure, head on down. She's doing great. She's in there with a friend who just stopped in a few minutes ago."

I waved goodbye to them all, then made my way to Anna's room, my mind trying to guess who the visitor might be. I walked through the open door into a room that looked more like a Pottery Barn ad than a hospital room. The muted earth tones radiated a peaceful, easy feeling, with pictures of beaches and sunrises scattered about. Fading golden light streamed in all around Anna, who was sitting up in bed wearing a Villanova T-shirt. Her guest sat in the chair next to the bed, her back to me, her dark hair in a long ponytail.

Anna saw me first and smiled. "Ah, Michael, you found me." She extended her arms. I made my way to her and gave her a hug and a kiss, then handed her my remaining bunch of flowers. "Oh, my, these are beautiful," she said. "And they smell wonderful. Just what this room needs."

I turned to the visitor, who had stood up. I was not sure what my facial expression was when she turned to look at me. "Got a bunch for me?" Susan asked.

"I'm all out for now, but I'll be sure to get more." I moved closer so we could hug. "You look fantastic. And if it's not too rude to ask, what are you doing here?"

"Oh, I was just telling Anna about how you called me a bitch." The women looked at each other and laughed as Susan poked my side. "Hey, come on, Michael, we're just kidding. I'm here doing some volunteer hours and wanted to stop and see Anna."

Anna continued, "It's so good to see Susan, and I sure am thankful to her for taking care of Nick last week. I can't even imagine what he was going through." She paused. "You know . . . with my turn for the worse and all." She held up her fingers to suggest quotes when she said "turn for the worse."

The three of us talked for about half an hour . . . about Nick, Anna's recovery, the baby, my job search, and Susan's recovery. Given what both these women had gone through, I was amazed at their smiles and positive focus on the future.

"Well, I've got to get going," Susan said. She stood at Anna's bedside and I noticed she really did look nice, her eyes clear and alert, her face lean and her smile easy. "I hope you'll let me come visit you and Nick and your new baby soon."

Anna smiled, holding out her arms to Susan, the flowers now lying on the table next to her bed. "Absolutely, it will be great to see you. And I'm so happy you're doing well with your recovery. I'll have you in my prayers."

Susan smiled and winked at Anna. "Thanks, I'll take them!" She turned to me, "Wanna walk me out?"

"Sure." I looked to Anna. "I'll be right back."

"Take your time."

Susan took my arm as we walked out of the room and to a small bench down the hall surrounded by green plants with white flowers, a small statue of Buddha nestled in the middle. "Can we just sit for a minute?" she asked, pulling me down to the bench next to her. She reached behind her head, pulling her ponytail straight out and then dropping it down her back.

"You look great. How are you?" I asked, not sure I wanted to get into a long conversation but trusting my intent in asking the question.

"You know, Michael, I'm doing really well. It's not easy, but I'm thankful for where I am. One day at a time is a good approach for me right now." I nodded as she took my hand. "It's just cool for me to get such a good feeling when I come here and help people. People I don't even know. I just feel so good. And I for sure don't miss the hangovers."

She looked at me with teary eyes. "I just want to thank you."

I shook my head. "For what?"

"For being in church that day when I stopped in. It feels like that was a long time ago."

I thought back to that day and the serendipity of our separate journeys that led us to be there together.

"Michael." She took my other hand in hers. "I was so close to going to get a drink when I found myself slowing down in front of St. John's. I don't really know how to say it other than that something . . . someone, was leading me there." She paused, pulling a tissue from her pocket and wiping her tears. "When I saw you there, I felt better, and the urge for a drink lessened." She stopped, her bottom lip quivering.

I hugged her shoulder. "It's OK, Susan. It's OK."

After a few deep breaths, she continued. "But then . . . then when you told me my dad's spirit was with me"—she smiled, squeezing my hands—"then I knew I could do this . . . I had to try to do this."

We stood and hugged for a long time. As we parted, I took her face in my hands, looking directly into her eyes. "Susan, believe this too, you are *doing* this. You are not just *trying*. We're not using that word try anymore . . . you *are* doing this! And I—for one—am so freaking proud of you. Keep going."

She smiled, unable to speak, and leaned in to kiss my cheek before turning and walking down the hall. I sat there alone, welcoming my tears.

After some time, I stood and headed back to Anna's room. She was reading *People* magazine when I came in, the cover showing a celebrity couple and their new baby. I noticed that her pregnancy was much more noticeable now. I guess I'd not been too focused on that the last few times I had been with her. She dropped the magazine in her lap, looking at me with a small smile.

I tilted my head sideways. "What?"

"What what?" she replied.

I laughed, responding, "Oh no, not this again. This 'what what?' must be a woman thing. I just went through this with my mom this morning."

She sat up in the bed. "And I love your mom; she's great. And it's no secret that we are the stronger communicators of the sexes."

I rolled my eyes, shuffling my feet in a fake stagger. "I'm not even going there."

She motioned for me to come closer. "Michael, thank you."

I was shocked by the tone she used. I can't explain it, but it was like she knew everything that had happened with me—or rather, me and Jay. *Shit, what do I say now? What do I do? I wish Jay was here.*

She was smiling. "It's alright. I know." She paused. "I understand."

I did my best to play dumb. "Know what?"

She pulled me to sit on the side of the bed, staring right into my eyes. "I know what you did. What you and Jay did. So I wanted to thank you."

I shook my head and laughed. "Yeah, the stronger communicators, my ass." Anna joined in my laughter and we hugged. Silence settled as we sat there, holding hands, looking at each other. An urge to speak came over me but faded quickly like a lit match in the wind. Anna laid her head back and closed her eyes. "I'm just gonna get a quick nap before Nick and our parents come back."

Anna fell asleep as the sky darkened beyond the windows. I put my head back in my chair and reached down, pulling the handle to extend the footrest. She was breathing easily. I watched her belly rise and fall, and smiled at my vision of that little person in there being out here soon enough. After a few minutes I turned as I heard voices growing louder from beyond the door. I hopped up and went out the door, placing my index finger over my lips at Nick and the others. The chatter ceased, and Nick motioned for me to head to the lounge, where there were several other people eating from fast food bags and wrappers, the smell of French fries in the air.

The parents settled at a table in the corner, both men being sure to pull the chairs out for their wives. Nick and I headed to some chairs near the window. "I sure am glad about what's been happening," he began, staring out toward the star-speckled night, his fingers fiddling with the stubble on his chin. "It's just so hard to get my head around sometimes." He looked to me. "It's almost like a miracle, right? I mean, the doctors are happy, but I can tell they're somewhat confused by what happened." He paused. "What do you think, buddy?"

I leaned forward in the chair, rubbing my hands on my thighs. "It sure is great. I was just sitting in there when you came back, and I was smiling at how healthy she looked, how peacefully she was resting, and I couldn't help but think about the baby.

"And it was good to see Susan; she's doing really good with her program and recovery. At first I was surprised when I saw her in Anna's room." I shifted in my chair. "I wasn't sure what was going on."

Nick laughed a bit. "Yeah, me too, when she showed up. But it was all good. She really is a great lady, and she's been through a lot too. I really feel like she's gonna be OK. I'll always be thankful for her helping me that night before you got back into town."

"Yep, she was good that night; and it all worked out." I hit Nick on his shoulder as I stood. "I gotta get rolling. I'm so glad Anna's doing well, and it looks like the worst is behind you."

"Yeah, me too," said Nick as we hugged and headed over to the parents for me to say goodbye. I stopped back by the Buddha statue on the way out, pulling my phone out and checking the time before I texted Jay.

> ME: Hey. I'm trusting all is good with you. How about a beer at Harry's?

> JAY: Sure, but only one.

> ME: Of course, only one Miller Lite – got it. I'll be there in about 15 minutes.

> JAY: 👍

CHAPTER 18

The Trust

Just trust yourself, then you will know how to live. – Johann Wolfgang Von Goethe

I was singing one of my favorite country songs on the drive to Harry's, a smile fixed on my face, and trust me, I was good with that. That smile dissolved instantly when I saw the black Range Rover in Harry's parking lot. I parked a few spots away and was making my way toward the front door when I saw Jon coming my way, dressed in saddle shoes, navy slacks and an expensive-looking golf pullover, and to top it off his hat was on backwards. *Why is he wearing that get-up on a Friday night in November?* I thought of trying to head across the lot, but he'd seen me, so I continued his way, noticing his swerving walk.

"Hey, Jon."

He smirked, pulling the keys from his pocket and pointing them at his car as the beep of the car unlocking was heard. "Oh, hey there, Michael. You here to put in an application?"

My self-talk began. *Oh, so this is how it's going to be. Stay calm, Michael, stay calm. But all I want to do is drop him right here. What an ass.* I took a deep breath, let my fists relax, shook my head and summoned a smile. "No, Jon, just heading in to see a friend."

I walked by him as he slid my way, our shoulders almost touching. I turned back at the sound of his slurred speech. "Listen, stay away from Jackie, or, trust me, I will kick your ass." I glanced away, then back to him with an "I'd love to see you do that." I stared until he turned and headed to his car. That's when I saw the words on the front of his hat: *Fair Oaks Turkey Open.* I'd forgotten the local elite course held a final tournament this late in the season for hard-core golfers.

As I opened the door to Harry's and started inside, I bumped into Jackie, who had rounded the corner at a fast pace. "Hey, hey, slow down there."

She never stopped walking. "Oh, hi, I gotta go," she said over her shoulder as I turned and followed. The Range Rover was parked out front. Jon looked at me through the side window. "Come on," he yelled to Jackie. "I'll forget what you said in there—let's just go home."

She shook her head, looked at me then back to him. "Jon, in a minute, but I'm driving."

"Yeah, yeah, whatever. Let's just go."

She turned to me, as Jesse and the huge Hawaiian bouncer, Akamu, came out the door. "Everything good here?" Jesse asked.

Jackie nodded. "Hey, Jesse. Yes, everything's fine. I'm driving him home in a minute." Jesse whispered something to the bouncer before going inside. Jackie turned back to me. "Sorry about this. I was going to call you to tell you how glad I was when I heard about Anna—it's such good news." She stopped as the sound of the horn came from the Rover. After an annoyed glance in Jon's direction, she said, "And I know why you didn't come over to my place the other night. I got it. Nick sure is lucky to have you as his friend."

"Thanks," I said, noticing that Jon had gotten out of the car and was leaning on the driver's side. "I think it's clear that we're both moving on . . . and in different directions." Her eyes filled as she leaned forward to kiss my cheek. She turned away. "And Jack?" I continued. She turned back. "You know I luv ya . . . always have, always will." She wiped a tear off her cheek and was about to turn when I heard Akamu yell, "Look out!"

I turned to see Jon's right hand swinging at my face and managed to pull my head back as his fist passed in front of my nose. He stumbled forward, then looked up, managing a half step toward me. I reacted instinctively and my fist landed squarely on the left side of his face, smashing his nose. A burst of blood instantly spread over his expensive white pullover, covering the Nike logo. He dropped to one knee as I backed away, fists raised, and heard Jackie yell, "Jonnnnnnn."

Akamu grabbed him under his arms and helped him to his feet as Jackie grabbed a towel from the car and came to his side, holding it to his nose, and pulling his head back. Akamu had him in an armlock and pushed him into the front passenger seat. He stood between me and the car as Jackie quickly made her way to the driver's side door. She shot me a glance before getting in and peeling away.

"You OK?" Akamu asked, his muscles rippling beneath his black *Harry's* T-shirt. "Good thing you were quick with that head move or you'd be the one with the bloody nose." He held out his hand for a slap.

"Yeah, yeah, I'm good. Thanks for the heads-up on that guy. I owe you one." I turned to the door, but had the feeling of someone watching me, so I turned toward the corner of the building where a small piece of the outdoor deck was visible. I smiled as I saw Jay standing there, holding up his two fingers in a peace sign. I shook my head and walked through the open door held by Akamu.

I went right to the men's room to calm down a bit and throw some water on my face. As I walked out, Jesse came over to me right away. "You good? Akamu just told me what happened."

"Hey, Jess. Yeah, I'm good. He's just a knucklehead, that guy."

"Asshole is more like it," he said. "Well, good on ya for dropping him. You know I'm a peaceful man, but evil cannot be tolerated." He winked, nodding toward the deck. "Go get Jay and come to the bar. You got a beer coming on me."

"Will do. Thanks, Jesse." I began walking toward the door, glancing to the empty pool table and thinking maybe Jay and I would shoot a few racks. Just as I was approaching the deck door, a tall man, wearing the same white Nike pullover as Jon, stood up from a booth and stepped right into my path. My calm demeanor vanished as I realized the guy was a friend of Jackie's dad. A few seconds later, I saw that her dad was there, too. He—also in the same pullover—was out of the booth and standing directly in front of me. "Hey, Michael. No job interviews today?"

I was not in the mood for any of Mr. Jennings' shit, and I took a step toward him. "You know what, Mr. Jennings?"

"What?"

"You all look real nice in your matching sweaters, and I'm guessing you probably cheated your way to another big win at some golf tournament." I noticed Jesse and Akamu walking up behind him. Mr. Jennings smiled and began to talk, but I cut him off quickly. "Save it. I just knocked your little puppet boy Jon on his ass out front, and last I looked, Jackie was driving him home as his nose was pouring blood all over his nice shirt." For the first time since I'd known this jerk, I noticed a trace of fear in his eyes as he swallowed. "And you know what? It felt good; and I'm just fine with doing the same thing to you."

His friend moved in next to Mr. Jennings in a show of solidarity just as Akamu grabbed both of them from behind. "OK, gentlemen, we've had enough here. I'm gonna walk you out of here and all will be good . . . or not. Your choice." That was the last I saw of Mr. Jennings for a long, long time.

I took a deep breath as Jay approached, wearing a slight grin. "Hey, Rocky, I'm ready any time for that beer you promised me." I just shook my head and laughed as we settled onto barstools. Jesse put a Miller Lite in front of each of us.

We both took a sip. I turned to Jay. "Was I wrong?"

"That's not my call."

"Just give me your opinion."

"Well. . . ." Jay turned to me. A silver cross hung around his neck where his denim shirt was open at the top. "In that case, I have a few thoughts. First, I trust you understand that if I said you were right . . . or wrong, then I'd be in judgment." I nodded. "When people are in judgment of others there is no progress. And while I certainly do not condone violence, I also realize Jon was going to punch you in the face."

I took another sip, trying to flex out the soreness in my right hand. "So it was OK?"

"Michael, again, my answer to this would be judgment of your actions. What I saw was another imperfection in life, an imperfection resulting from anger, too much drink, and maybe some insecurities showing up on Jon's part." He smiled at an older couple leaving their booth.

"Well, I was feeling kind of bad that I hit Jon, but he had it coming. I don't like to fight. But I was ready to knock Jackie's dad on his ass, too." I chuckled to myself. "That would have gone over really well with Jackie."

Jay turned his head sideways, rolling his eyes.

He motioned to Jesse and ordered some wings and nachos. While we waited for the food, we turned to the TV to watch the previews of the weekend college football games.

While the sportscasters prattled on, I pondered my next question, one I'd thought about a lot recently. I took a deep breath and asked it. "So now what?"

A waitress brought the food and plates to us.

"Now? Now we enjoy our beer and food." Jay said. "Sound good?"

I took a swig, placing my bottle on the damp bar napkin. "Yes, but you know what I mean. Is there anything else we . . . I mean, you, need to do for Anna? Or the baby? And what about Dr. Chelson and Dr. Ali?"

"No, there is nothing else to do. It is done."

"But Anna knows. She told me."

Jay looked to me from the TV. "Yes, and it will be OK."

"But what if she tells Nick? Or the doctors?"

"Michael, the doctors are fine people and fine physicians, but their thoughts may sometimes be too limited by the facts." Jay took a sip of beer, then wiped his face with a napkin. He grabbed another wing, dipping it into the blue cheese, then turned to me and winked. "The Divine is not limited by facts."

"But what if something happens?"

"Like what?" Jay responded.

I was confused now, thinking way too fast. "I don't know. I just hope everything is going to be alright, you know, work out."

"I see. Well, you can hope, or then again maybe you could just choose to focus on one word—begins and ends with T."

I winced. "Five letters," he offered. It came to me.

"Trust," I said. Jay nodded, holding up his thumb as he grabbed another wing.

I smiled. "Yes, trust. But what then have I always learned about faith, hope and love. . . ."

"And the greatest of these is love," Jay interrupted.

"Right. But why isn't it faith, trust, and love?"

"Not really sure," Jay said. "But it's good as faith, hope and love. But then again faith is really a belief without proof." I nodded. "So that is where trust is connected. For me, faith is the noun, and trust is the verb. Trust is what you do."

I put the wing I was about to eat on my plate. "Right. We say, 'In God we *trust*,' not '*hope*.' I guess you've offered me a different way to look at it." My mind slowed. "What about us? Are you staying around? Will I see you again? I have a strange feeling that our time is coming to an end, like what was meant to be is done."

"Well, that depends on how you define 'see.' We may not be together, like we have been and are now, but I'm always here with you . . . even if you cannot see me."

Just then I felt a smack on the back that caused alarm as I turned. My mood lightened as I saw my friend Eric. "Hey, brother, how are you? Long time since we last saw one another." He said as I stood and we hugged. He looked to Jay. "Sorry to interrupt; just wanted to say hi to my old buddy. It's been a lot of years since we first met at altar server training."

"It sure has been. Damn, you look great." I turned to Jay. "Jay, this is my old friend, Eric. Eric, Jay." The two shook hands as I continued, "What's up? How are you?"

Eric went on to tell me that he had moved to L.A. for a while, was working in the financial services field and had just moved back a few months ago with his wife and baby daughter to run the regional office for his company. Eric and I had been real close through high school, and then he played football at a college in the same league as mine, so we'd work out in the summer a bit, and see each other at our games and over the holidays. His parents were always at Mass and had become friendly with my mom.

After a few minutes, we exchanged numbers and agreed to get together for dinner soon. "I guess I'll see you at Mass as well."

Eric frowned, shaking his head. "No, probably not. I've not been going. Sort of feeling that the Church really screwed up Jesus' message. It just doesn't work for me anymore." He shook Jay's hand in a parting gesture. I suppressed laughter at the cosmic humor of whose hand he was shaking given his last statement.

Jay and I finished our beers and food and I ordered another Miller Lite.

"Sure you don't want another?" I asked Jay.

"Nope. You know me. Just one."

"Yep, I know. How come?" I caught my accusing tone. "Just asking."

"I choose to enjoy a cold Miller Lite from time to time; and I choose not to have my thoughts influenced by too much alcohol . . . so it works for me to have just one." He sipped from the glass of water Jesse had, as usual, placed in front of him.

"Got it."

He winked. "Although there was this wedding a long time ago with some wine."

I smiled, remembering my Bible study, then switched topics. "Jay, do you run into people like Eric a lot? I'm guessing a lot of people have the same view as him." I paused. "And I mean this respectfully, but they also think that the church has screwed up the message." I just shook my head. "Forgive me, really can't believe I'm telling *you* this. How about I close the tab and we sit outside for a few minutes next to the fire pits?"

"Sure," said Jay as he stood, putting on his zip-up hoodie. "I'll go get us two seats."

I called Jesse, asking for the check. He showed up a minute later with the check, a beer, and a steaming mug topped with whipped cream. "What's this?"

Jesse smiled and winked, "Jay loves a hot chocolate nightcap." He paused as he looked outside to the deck, causing me to do so as well, and we saw Jay settling into a chair in the corner. "Especially when he's out in nature . . . as he puts it." We laughed and I left some money on the bar, then grabbed the drinks and headed to the deck.

The deck was crowded with people in sweaters and fleece jackets warding off the chill. The faces were lit from the glow of the fires and phones. I was not surprised Jay had settled around the one fire pit on the deck that had just two chairs, almost as if he knew we needed some privacy for our discussion of Eric's testimony.

"Ah, that Jesse is a fine man." Jay took the steaming mug from me and set it on the tile ledge of the fire pit not far from the steady flame.

I leaned forward, placing my palms near the fire and rubbing my hands. "What do you think about Eric and lots of other people saying that the church screwed up your message? I've struggled with my faith recently, and sometimes I feel a little like Eric. There are so many stories lately about the church and its leaders getting into trouble."

I took a sip of beer. "So many times I've been at Mass and the priest doesn't give a good message in his sermon. A lot of times it's about money, or they're talking about the people who aren't even there at Mass."

Jay blew on his drink before taking a sip and holding the mug between both hands as it rested on his knee. "It's OK, Michael. Eric's claim is a valid one. Perhaps the answer—if there is one—lies in what you just said." He paused as I shook my head in confusion. "You just said the church and its leaders screwed up my message. You see, these are two different issues and must be viewed that way. The church, the institution, is made up of people, and you and I both know people are imperfect. However, I guarantee the integrity of the message—despite the imperfections of the human messengers."

I was locked onto Jay, pulled by his words. He looked away to the fire, then back to me. "Like I said to a friend of mine long ago, 'You are Peter and upon this rock I will build my Church, and the gates of Hell will not prevail against it.'"

"So that's it? We just accept the fact that people aren't perfect, and then let our spiritual life suffer?"

"No, not necessarily." Jay pulled the hood over his head. "I'd encourage you and others to think about this: Consider the community of believers, of Christians left behind after my death. They were fallible human beings, just average people. I didn't leave my message in the hands of the educated, or the rulers, or the Roman leaders. I did not intend to leave my message to the educated and wealthy and influential of the day. I left it in the hearts and minds and hands of those who would struggle to realize our ultimate goal."

Jay's insights made sense, although I hadn't really looked at the Church and faith that way before. "What's the ultimate goal?" I asked.

"Not so fast," Jay said as a group of young people around the fire pit next to us laughed in unison. "Let's spend some more time on the message. What do you think the 'message' is that Eric and so many others believe is screwed up?"

I paused, stretching my neck from side to side. "Man, Jay, this is getting deep. I guess the message is what you talked about and taught over 2,000 years ago. You know, the Ten Commandments, and"—I struggled to go on—"and the beatitudes.

"I guess the message is just what you told us about the way to live," I added. "To live according to your teachings."

"OK, good. So how do you see that message being screwed up?"

I put my beer down on the slate next to my seat and leaned in. "I guess I see it when the priests are not real good at preaching, and when they talk about money and all that." Jay nodded as I paused, trying to decide whether to say what I was thinking. He looked at me, smiling, and I felt as though he knew my thinking. "Do you know what I'm gonna say next?"

"Maybe. Try me."

"Ok, here goes. Everywhere we look there are people being treated poorly just because they are who they are. You know—how they live, where they come from, their economic and social status. And they're treated poorly, sometimes by Christians."

Jay placed his mug back on the tile ledge and moved in close, his eyes misty. "Michael, the sins—and the crimes—that have been committed by people, by priests, deeply saddens me. Many lives have been inflicted with great suffering and pain. There's just been so much evil and hate and judgment and greed; thankfully the Spirit's strength has come to many of these people on their journey. I offer to the faithful that, again, we're not perfect. But considering the challenges of the Church throughout history, and certainly recently, my message remains strong. We must bring evildoers to justice, and we must remain connected to the message." Jay looked through the flames into my eyes. "We, the Church here on earth, must enter into and strengthen our relationships with all our sisters and brothers. We must generate much more compassion, respect, understanding and quite simply . . . love."

"Not so easy," I said.

"Yes, life is not easy. We're all in the struggle to continue finding our place in the Church and strengthening our loving relationship with God."

I nodded, recalling my conversation with Father Green about God being both external and internal within us. "Yeah, I was talking with a priest, Father Green, at breakfast with my mom a few months ago, and we had the conversation about the external God we pray to and the same God that is within each of us that we must connect with."

Jay smiled, "Oh, yes, Matthew, a wonderful man and priest. He references John, who wrote, 'On that day, you will know that you are in me and I am in you.' "

"You know him?" I had no sooner got this out than I continued as Jay smiled. "Yes, sorry, of course you know him."

Jay looked at me. "So, Michael, I'm leaving soon, and you'll not see me for a while. Anna and the baby are doing well."

I objected. "No, you can't leave yet. What if something happens? Can't you just wait until the baby is born?"

Jay shook his head. "Trust, Michael, trust." I took a deep breath. Jay continued, "A few minutes ago you were referencing my message— the one so many think has been screwed up." I nodded. "And yes, my teachings about the Commandments and the Beatitudes and through- out all the parables are part of the message.

" Do you know what organ is the first one formed in the embryo as the cells begin to divide and multiply?" Jay asked. I shook my head, not sure if I knew that or not.

"Our heart." Jay touched his chest gently.

I just sat there as a peaceful feeling permeated my body, savoring my last few minutes with my friend. "Go on Jay, please."

"Michael, my message is not screwed up at all, as Eric chooses to state it. People are coming too much from their brain—their head—in strengthening their relationship with me and living a Christian life." He paused. The deck seemed to take on a momentary silence. "They must come from their hearts. They must lead with love." I realized I was holding my breath, and let it out. "Michael, my message is strong. It's continued for more than 2,000 years, and will continue on. The Church is the organization around the message. It is made up of people— imperfect people—people who struggle and fail."

"So they should come back to the Church?" I asked, feeling like a reporter wrapping up an interview.

Jay let that question sit for a moment, then turned to me and spoke slowly. "They should come back to the message. The rest will follow."

We sat in silence as Jay finished his hot chocolate and I pondered the immense emotion I was feeling from Jay's simple—yet profound—message.

"Before we leave, what's the ultimate goal you mentioned earlier?"

"Yes, thank you for asking. Our spirituality in this world will be fully realized not through a few individuals, but when all individuals lead with love and form a strong, consistent unit of humanity." He stared into the flames, and then looked into my eyes. "What many refer to as the mystical body of Christ." I sat there, unable to move or speak. "This will happen when people both have their faith not only in me, but also the faith of me."

I shook my head, confused. "I have faith in you, but what do you mean to have the faith *of* you?"

"I mean to have the same faith that I have in the will of my Father in Heaven."

"But that's one and the same, isn't it? I mean, you and He are one . . . with the Spirit, right?"

"Yes and no. I came as a human to show how to be human and have that faithful relationship with God. We all need to have that same faith."

After a few minutes I asked, "Jeez, when will that happen?"

"Not sure. Just do your part in moving it all in that direction. Sound good?"

I nodded slowly, my body filled with a peaceful energy. "I get that you're leaving, and I just wanted to say that this whole thing has. . ." Jay put his index finger to his lips, suggesting I stop talking.

"I know," he said, a smile spreading on his face, the reflection of the flames bounding off his misty eyes.

"OK, OK, but can I ask you just one more question?"

"Sure."

"You said to me once when we were in the hospital"—I shook my head, grinning—"when we were invisible, that there are others. Do you mean angels? People who have passed and continue to come back? Are there really others?"

I tightened up as a strong hand grabbed the back of my neck, then slid over my shoulder and down my arm. It was Akamu.

"Ah, perfect timing," said Jay. "Akamu, my friend, Michael here was just asking about the others, and do they exist. What do you think?'

Akamu hugged me tightly, his muscles solid, and looked at me. "Ha ha, yes, Michael, my brother . . . we are here." He winked and made his way off the deck, dragging two trashcans behind him.

"Your face right now is priceless," said Jay with a laugh.

I stammered, "What? Really? Akamu?"

He nodded. "Google the meaning of his Hawaiian name." He stood. "Come on, walk me to my car."

I stood and said, "Sure. I'm getting out of here too."

As we approached the shiny black Camaro, Jay put his arm over my shoulder. "Michael, you're a fine man. Keep your faith, *be your faith*, and trust that I'll protect you sometimes and provide you strength in others. And above all"—he gave me a hug then separated before finishing—"lead with love."

"I will. Thank you for everything. Will I ever see you again?"

"I'm here, I'm around . . . always." My eyes filled as I reflected on the months since I'd first met him in Harry's and Brew Ha Ha. *What an amazing gift I'd received. It would be a better world if everyone could meet Him.*

Jay was about to get into his car when I called his name. "Hey, Jay, I was just thinking about if someone were to ask me what I did today."

Jay looked at me. "And?"

I paused before responding. "I'd tell them I met Jesus for a Miller Lite." As I turned and walked to my Jeep, I said to myself, *Yeah, that's what I'm gonna say.*

A Mere Breath

Man is like a mere breath; His days are like a passing shadow. - Psalm 144:4

I slept well that night, not rousing until early morning when I heard a knock at my bedroom door and the sound of my mom's unsteady voice. "Michael, Michael, wake up. I need you." I jumped out of bed as my mom opened the door. She turned and headed for the stairs, yelling back to me, "I don't know what's going on, but you need to come down right away."

"Mom, Mom, slow down," I said as I hurried after her. "Is everything OK?"

"I'm not sure, you'll have to see for yourself."

She led me through the living room and out the front door. The chill in the air hit me in my face as my bare feet felt the cold of the driveway. I stood, mouth open, not able to make sense of what I was seeing. There in the driveway, shining like an 8-ball on a pool table, was a black Camaro convertible. "Come here, look!" my mom shouted. She was pointing through the windshield. "There's an envelope on the dash with your name on it."

As I walked to the car, I noticed our old neighbor across the street, Mr. Whitcomb, standing on his front porch to see what all the excitement was about. I opened the door, slid in behind the wheel, and picked up the envelope. "What is it? What does it say?" my mom prompted.

"Mom, OK. Give me a minute." I opened and read the short note:

Michael - Take care of her.

Peace.

There was a folded paper in the envelope. I pulled it out and saw that the title to the car was in my name. Tucked into the paper was an insurance card with all my information on it. "Well, Mom, it looks like this is mine now."

"What?" she yelled. "A car just shows up, a real nice car too, in our driveway and now you say it's yours?"

I walked to Mom and gave her a hug. "Let's go in and get some tea. I'll explain everything." She reluctantly agreed, nervously looking around to see if this was some kind of practical joke. We walked arm in arm as my mind raced to figure out what I was going to say. Inside, as we sipped tea, I told her about Jay, staying in the truth but leaving out many of the details. I simply said he was a guy I'd become friends with who was very blessed with abundance (I know what you're thinking, but it's true, right?) and who was going away and wanted me to have his car. Mom was not real comfortable with the whole thing, but I gave her a hug and assured her that it was all going to be OK, and for her to trust me. I smiled to myself when I said "trust."

# # #

Twenty-five years sounds like a long time. But if you're over 40, you know it goes by in a flash. It was spring and the sun that was coming up over the Rockies hit my face as the top came down on my 25-year-old Camaro. I made a quick trip to the coffee shop before heading back home to get ready for a morning meeting. My mom's been gone now for 10 years, dying quickly and way too soon from an aggressive disease that ravaged her body. I'm thankful that she did visit me here often for some wonderful days on the slopes of Breckenridge, Vail, and Aspen. Her courage did not surprise me during the illness; she remained strong in her faith, continuing to serve the Church community and many others through her volunteer efforts. Her funeral was a tough day for me, although the comments from friends and family about my talk that day provided a wonderful comfort.

I went into my office intending to write in my journal but instead ended up staring out at the foothills of the Rocky Mountains. I had written six words: *Where have all the years gone?* I miss my mom every day and am always thankful for the wonderful relationship and friendship we had. As you can tell, I still have the Camaro and it's still shiny and black. I wish I could say the same for my hair, but it's more of a soft gray now. I came close to selling the car once, but I thought back to my mom's reaction that morning after Jay left it in our driveway, and I laughed out loud and thought, *I gotta keep this car forever.*

Anna recovered from her cancer and has lived a healthy life. She and Nick have three kids, two in college and one already engaged and getting married next year. They came out last year for their 25th anniversary, and we had a lot of fun celebrating in Aspen for a few days, skiing and enjoying some wonderful meals. I'm pretty sure they have the best kind of marriage. I've seen too many marriages fail, or see couples just kind of go through the motions when they don't work on being best friends. I know it sounds romantic for me to say this, but I do firmly believe they have the best kind of basis for a long, loving, resilient marriage . . . being best friends.

Susan went on to become an advocate for addiction and people in recovery, and she and I have stayed in touch. She married, went back to school for her master's and doctorate, and has written some wonderful books—one which actually was made into a movie and nominated for an Oscar. It didn't win, but I was so proud to catch her TV interviews leading up to the awards ceremony. I never did tell her that "the guy in the orange sweatshirt" was her dad pushing her down in the parking lot so she didn't get into her car. Sometimes I think she probably knows.

I still see Sheila from time to time when I head back east and visit with Nick and Anna. She's remained single, very close with Nick and Anna, and enjoys being an "aunt" to their kids, and a wonderful nurse.

Predictably, Jackie and I didn't end up together. She married Jon a few years after he and I had our little mishap—I guess I can call it that—in front of Harry's. She actually stopped by my work a few years ago. She'd emailed, saying she and her family were headed to Vail and would it be OK if she stopped by my office to say hi and have a quick visit. I replied that would be wonderful.

The day of the visit, I was in my office preparing for an upcoming meeting. I'd skipped breakfast as my stomach was queasy (even after nearly a quarter century).

My assistant had popped her head in and said that Jackie was here with another man and two boys. I'd stood and made my way to the door just as she entered, looking beautiful in jeans, black boots and a black sweater. Her hair was shoulder length, with wisps of gray; she easily could have passed for an aging supermodel. She still smelled the same.

She'd introduced me to her sons, who'd inherited more of her looks than Jon's, and they'd all settled into chairs in my office. My assistant had said that the man was in the men's room and she'd show him in shortly.

We'd been talking about their trip to Vail and the accommodations and snow conditions, when a man appeared in the doorway. It was not Jon, as I'd expected. It took a moment for me to recognize him. "Well, hello, Mr. Jennings." I'd stood and extended my hand, but he'd ignored it and given me a warm embrace.

"Hello, Michael," he'd said. "It's really nice to see you after all this time. You look great." I decided he must be approaching 80 years old, but he was in good shape, standing straight and tall and walking steadily. His shoulders looked strong, and other than a slight belly and gray hair, he looked quite the same. "I can see on your face that I'm probably the last person you expected to see." He'd laughed.

"You can say that again," I had replied. "It's nice to see you, and I'm glad you're well." We'd chatted for about 15 minutes, then Mr. Jennings had put his hands on the boys' shoulders. "Let's say goodbye here and run over to Starbucks before we jump in the car. Your mom and Michael probably want a few minutes alone." The boys had stood, shaken my hand and told their mom they'd see her downstairs. I'd smiled when they'd both stopped to give her a kiss on her cheek.

Mr. Jennings had come to me and extended his hand. "Michael, thanks for letting us stop by. One thing I've learned throughout my life is that you cannot go back to the past." He'd paused, looking to Jackie and then back to me. "But you can recover from it. You're a real good man, Michael. You always have been, and I was wrong for treating you the way I did so many years ago. Take care and God bless." He'd pulled me in for another hug.

"God bless you too, Mr. Jennings. And thank you." He'd left with the boys and I'd settled into the chair next to Jackie.

She had smiled. "Guess you didn't see that coming?"

"Not at all," I'd replied, with an eye roll and laughter.

"Well, he wanted to come see you. He sure has changed a lot since my mom died. They had a wonderful relationship, and he sure loved her. I kind of think losing her was a tragedy that shifted his perspective. I'm sure my mom's up there, and happy to have a part in that; I remember many talks with her about Dad's treatment of others. I'm just proud of him for it."

"Right," I'd said. "Never too late to hold up the mirror to ourselves and see where we might have some opportunity." We'd talked a few minutes then she'd taken my hands.

"Michael, I'm not sure if you heard or not, but Jon and I got divorced about four years ago. He'd had an affair when the boys were much younger, but we'd worked through it, and I guess I thought he'd change." Her eyes had welled up as she continued. "I guess the second one, with his ex-fiancée, you remember the one with the big—"

I'd interrupted before she could finish. "Oh yes, I remember her. I'm sorry, Jackie."

"Thanks, but it's OK and I'm OK. If I had to guess, there were more. But that one kind of made me realize the change I had hoped for was not going to happen." She'd chuckled through her sniffles. "My dad was ready to knock him on his ass like you did that day."

I'd squeezed her hands tightly, grabbed a tissue from the box on the coffee table and laughed a bit with her. It had felt good. She'd smiled when she'd seen me notice a very familiar silver necklace around her neck. I'd simply said, "Peace, right?" She'd nodded and hugged me as we stood, chatted a few more minutes, and agreed to stay in touch. I'd walked her to the elevator. We'd smiled at each other as the doors came together, separating us yet again.

It feels like that meeting happened yesterday but it was two years ago. As I reflect on life, I shake my head and laugh at how quickly it truly does pass. Mine has been like many . . . good times, bad times, confusing times, joyful times, times of conviction, and times of ambiguity. Ryan, my Marine friend, and I have become very close. I'll always remember his talk when we'd met in front of his office and he said to me, "Michael, we all get hit . . . just in different ways."

As for me? Well, it's been good. I worked the TV thing for a few years and got quite successful. As I'd hoped, it allowed me to stay connected with football but also spend more time in Pennsylvania and work in the community in my hometown since I didn't have to move around as much. It was the best of both worlds.

Then I went on a ski trip to Denver with some friends . . . and ended up moving here. Something about the mountains seemed to be beckoning me. I left my TV job, returned to school, and made a few what might be called wrong turns, but I figured it out and now all is good. I absolutely love my job—challenges and all.

While I never married, I do have a special woman in my life whom I've known for almost 20 years now, and it's pretty safe to say she's one of my best friends . . . maybe even tied with Nick. Her name is Ellen Grace, and she's the Executive Director of a large global non-profit based here in Denver. I actually had a wonderful dinner at her home last night with her husband and four children.

All in all, I'm thankful for the many blessings—and struggles— over these past 25 years, and I look forward to the next 25, or however many I'm blessed with.

I was thinking about this just the other day when I was in my church, the Cathedral of the Immaculate Conception, with some others. It was the end of Mass and I raised my hands from my place on the altar.

I gazed out at our wonderful parishioners and visitors and said, "Go in peace to love and serve the Lord." And they responded, "Thanks be to God" as soft music filled the massive church. Peace.

CPSIA information can be obtained
at www.ICGtesting.com
Printed in the USA
LVHW03s1845200918
590799LV00011B/980/P